YOUR STUDENT RESEARCH PROJECT

To A, J, M and N, the ladies in my life

Your Student Research Project

MARTIN LUCK

Gower

Published by
Gower Publishing Limited
Gower House
Croft Road
Aldershot
Hampshire GU11 3HR
England

Gower
Old Post Road
Brookfield
Vermont 05036
USA

British Library Cataloguing in Publication Data
Luck, Martin
    Your student research project
    1. Research – Methodology – Handbooks, manuals, etc.
    2. Dissertations, Academic
    I. Title
    001.4'024375

ISBN 0 566 08213 6

Typeset in Century Schoolbook by IML Typographers, Chester and printed in Great Britain by The University Press, Cambridge

CONTENTS

LIST OF FIGURES

LIST OF TABLES

LIST OF BOXES

ACKNOWLEDGEMENTS

I am indebted to many friends and colleagues who helped make this book possible, including:

Sue Drew, Margaret Herrington, Kate Millar and Alistair Stott for discussion and advice on specific areas of the text.

Roni Brown, Roger Catchpole, Rob Clarke, Patrick Coldstream, Ian Drummond, Chrissie Gibson, Helen Henry, Morag Hunter, Paul Hyland, Andrew Illius, Brian Morris, Mike Riddle, Angela Smallwood, Debbie Sparkes and Mr A Woolley for unknowingly contributing ideas during talks and discussions.

The undergraduate students, individually remembered but too numerous to list, who over the years have carried out research projects and obtained degrees in spite of my supervision.

Martin Luck

INTRODUCTION

This book is designed to help you to get the most out of one particular part of your degree studies. Your research project or dissertation (Box 1.1) will be a major item in your final level of university study, but it amounts to a new experience within your academic career. It requires new personal skills, more self-confidence and a different mindset compared with anything you have done before.

Over the last few semesters, besides attending the formal parts of your course (lectures, seminars, tutorials, etc.), you have almost certainly already experienced several different types of self-directed study. These include things like essays, surveys, lab classes, workshops, mini-projects, etc. So by now you are quite skilful in managing your time, meeting deadlines and putting in the effort required to make a success of your coursework.

Now you are being asked to do an in-depth investigation to complete your studies. You will have to concentrate, by yourself, on a single, specialized topic within your main field of interest. The focus will change. You will need to work at a level of detail that you have not experienced before. You will have to be self-motivated and self-critical. New demands will be made on your time and on your powers of concentration, understanding and judgement. The pattern and intensity of life are about to change, radically.

You saw this coming, of course, and you're probably excited to be getting on with it at last. But, there are still only 25 hours in a day and your other modules continue to demand their share of your attention. The end of your course isn't that far off, so there's also job-hunting to be done. And you want to do yourself justice by getting a good degree.

This book shows you how to cope with your project and make a success of your studies. It aims:

❐   to be a practical guide to undergraduate project work within the framework of your degree course;

❐   to show you how to squeeze maximum value from the effort you put in;

❐   to enable you to recognize how you have changed in the process;

❐   to encourage you to exploit the skills and experience you have gained.

◼ WHY ANOTHER BOOK ON RESEARCH METHODS?

Your library, and perhaps your own bookshelf, holds other student study guides. You will also find in your library or bookshop several books on research methods. These volumes contain much wisdom but may not be quite what you are looking for. Many of the study guides you have seen are probably aimed at degree work in general and may say little about extended project or research work. At the other end of the scale, there are many research guides aimed at postgraduate students who are about to embark on an academic career. These students have rather different requirements from you, not least because they can afford to be totally focused on one thing and have a much longer time-scale within which to work. A few research guides, such as some of those listed in the Bibliography, are aimed at undergraduate rather than research students and are thoroughly recommended. They offer plenty of detailed advice, sometimes within the context of a single discipline area, and often delve into the theory of research methods.

This book takes a slightly different approach from most others because it tries to consider the research project in context. In other words, it expects you to be concerned not only with the process of research itself but also with how to cope with a project alongside the other components of your degree course. It concentrates on practical advice and ideas but gives thought to how you will manage your work within a crowded and exciting life.

◼ WHAT ABOUT SKILLS?

Many books on study skills include practical exercises of one kind or another designed to make you reflect on or develop particular abilities and aptitudes. These exercises can be very effective and you should not

Box 1.1   What are we talking about?

The terms **research project** and **dissertation** are used more or less inter-changeably throughout this book. They refer to *investigative learning activities*, also variously described as **reports, inquiries, theses, extended studies**, etc.

'Dissertation' and 'thesis' are frequently used simply to describe the final printed and bound product resulting from a research project. Sometimes 'dissertation' implies an essentially library-based rather than experiment- or survey-based investigation. The terminology varies between universities, even between departments. Different subject areas have their own traditions of usage.

It is difficult to come up with a common set of criteria, and definitions are unhelpful if they are too restrictive or exclusive. Nevertheless, whatever it is called, it will comprise a process (doing the work) and an outcome (report or product) and should have many of the following characteristics:

❒   Study in depth
❒   Originality
❒   Gestation of ideas
❒   Review or re-appraisal of existing knowledge
❒   Re-evaluation of current hypotheses, assumptions, procedures or working practices
❒   Contribution of new ideas or interpretations
❒   Exercise of critical faculties
❒   Input of personal endeavour
❒   Production of a structured, written report

Most importantly, it involves **research**. This, again, is a term to be used loosely. It encompasses everything from, for example, the molecular sequence analysis of a newly discovered gene, through a survey of public attitudes to censorship, to a textual comparison of all existing published editions of *Hamlet*. Each of these, in its own peculiar way, requires the origi-nal input of the researcher. Each will deliver something creative and new and interesting.

Even the most sedentary (and apparently often re-worked) literature survey is a process of original research since it involves the seeking out, selection and evaluation of information in a way which is unique to the researcher and can never have been done before. Collating, reviewing and imposing structure on an existing body of knowledge is as valuable as contributing a new piece of information.

hesitate to use them if you think they will help. Such exercises, how-ever, are often meant to be carried out in isolation from the real work you need to do: you end up with the desired skill but little or nothing to show by way of progress in the task itself. The exercises and examples in this book have been carefully designed so that their outcomes will be of **direct** practical use to you, either in doing an effective piece of study or in improving the quality of the final presentation.

CONTEXT

It would be difficult, probably impossible, to create a book of advice on any aspect of university study which is equally applicable to all aca-demic disciplines. The different subject areas offer such a wide variety of experience that no single book can hope to cater for all. Furthermore, departments and courses vary enormously in their expectations of students, including the extent to which they include research work within the final degree programme. This book is intended to be of use to you whatever your area of study but it inevitably contains material which you will not find appropriate. All advice is context sensitive and the use you are able to make of what this book offers will depend on your own background, needs and experiences.

My background is in the natural sciences. You will rapidly discern this from the style and content of the book, particularly if you are from a non-science background. For example, in the sections on project plan-ning and design, there is some bias towards 'experimental' methods, hypothesis testing, numerical analysis and other pure science approaches to research. The book is not intended to be exclusive, how-ever, and some effort has been made to make the bulk of its content relevant to all students who find themselves engaged in research for the first time. If certain sections seem to be out of step with what you are doing, feel free to skip them or read between the lines. (Students in arts, social sciences and education may in particular wish to consult books which deal directly with the research methods of their own fields such as Allison *et al.* (1996), Bell (1993), Berry (1994) and others listed in the Bibliography.) Be aware, however, that successful and produc-tive research has some common features whatever the discipline. There is often much to be gained by trying to appreciate how others approach it.

◼ LOOKING AHEAD

The process of doing your research can be divided up into several stages:

Stage 1: Thinking about it

Understanding the reasons for doing a research project, its potential benefits for you and how best to fit it into a busy degree course.

Stage 2: Planning it

Deciding which project to do, finding a supervisor, designing the project, asking the right questions and managing your efforts effectively.

Stage 3: Doing it

Taking a productive approach to your work, reading the literature, interacting with your supervisor and making the most of your opportunities.

Stage 4: Presenting it

Writing up the dissertation and presenting it for assessment.

Stage 5: Shouting about it

Telling the world about what you have done, realizing how you have changed as a person, and exploiting the skills you have developed (for example, to get a decent job).

This book is divided that way too. If you are looking at the book for the first time, it is likely that you are at Stage 1. The stages overlap in a way that book sections cannot, so once you get going you will have to dip into the chapters as you need them.

In summary, this book aims to put your research project in the correct perspective. Its tone is intended to be reflective as well as advisory. It encourages you to be enthusiastic but to keep your total workload in balance. It expects you to get completely immersed in the subject of the project but to keep your head above the waves and to remain in sight of land. Above all, it aims to help you keep track of where you are heading and to make the right preparations for the future.

Your project is a unique opportunity for you to sample the delights and frustrations of research, to experience the intensity of the investigative process and the excitements of discovery. Carrying out your project work will force you to think independently and move beyond any passive acceptance of the knowledge and beliefs of others. Your reaction to all this will be a personal one and cannot be predicted: you may find it totally enthralling and decide to make research your career vocation or you may feel like writing 'NEVER AGAIN' on the nearest motorway bridge. Whatever your experience and whatever you decide for the future, doing your own research will change your perception of life, your view of yourself and your assessment of your capabilities.

THINKING ABOUT IT

CHAPTER

2

MOTIVATION AND SKILLS

Your project is probably an obligatory part of your course. Since you have little choice, you may not have thought very much about why you are doing it. In fact, it is there for several different reasons, some of which you would recognize as personally valuable. Identifying these can help you to be properly motivated for the work. When you have finished your research, when the dissertation is finally printed, bound and submitted, you might want to reflect on what you have achieved and decide whether those reasons were valid.

TYPES OF MOTIVATION

Students have a number of different kinds of motivation for studying and learning (Table 2.1). Looking at the table, you can probably identify several or all of the reasons why you came to university in the first place and why you ended up studying the course you are now on. Not all of these reasons were necessarily positive and your motives may well have changed as your course developed.

Your motivation for project work may be extrinsic:

- 'It is an obligatory part of the course.'
- 'I need the experience to get a job.'

or intrinsic:

- 'It's something I've always wanted to do.'
- 'Now is my chance to study the subject properly'.

or achievement-driven:

❏   'I want to show what I'm really capable of.'
❏   'I think I'm capable of getting a really good degree.'

or a combination of these. As with the rest of your studies, your motivation for research may change, especially as you become more deeply involved and interested in the subject. Some students see the project as the natural continuation of a process which began when they left school: an increasing independence based on self-motivation, self-reliance and the discipline of having to manage one's own time and effort.

Table 2.1 Types of student motivation	
Type of motivation	*Characteristics*
Extrinsic	Driven from outside yourself
	Focuses on the satisfactory completion of the course
	Strongly influenced by external pressures and rewards
	Regards the work as a means to an end
	Can be driven by fear of failure
Intrinsic	Driven from inside yourself
	Reflects a personal goal
	Originates from an interest in the subject area
	Requires personal involvement with the work
	Depends on feelings of competence and self-confidence
Achievement-driven	Driven by ambition
	Focuses on personal levels of achievement
	Depends on time-management and organized study
	Regards tasks as personal challenges
	Can be competitive

■ WHY DO THEY WANT ME TO DO A RESEARCH PROJECT?

There are several answers to this question, to do with philosophy, practicality, exploitation and hedonism (Figure 2.1).

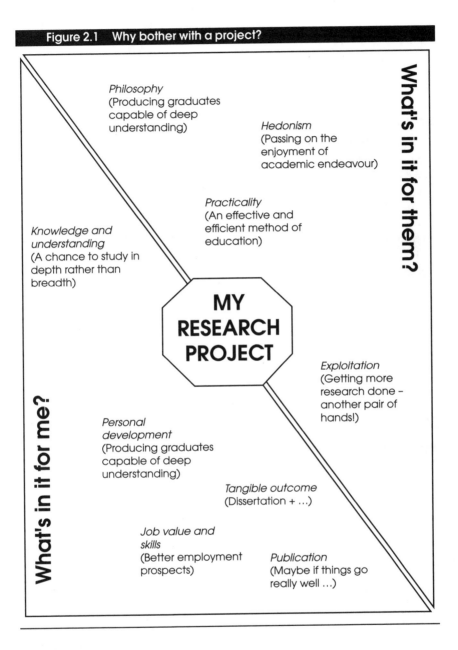

Figure 2.1   Why bother with a project?

1.   Philosophy

When you graduate, the letters of your degree will signify to the world that you have a level of knowledge, understanding and expertise not common among the rest of the population. That should make you feel good and encourage you to do well. But how certain is your knowledge?

How much do you really understand? How deep is your comprehension? What kind of an expert are you?

Your engineering degree may enable you to design bridges but you know well enough that the calculations for stress and strain contain approximations. Studying social history might allow you to explain the effects of new technology on the exploitation of manual labour, but you know as well as anyone that economic revolutions are largely a matter of subjective interpretation. In short, what you learn at university is flaky and uncertain. The received wisdom is full of generalizations, dates rapidly and has always to be questioned.

By getting you to do a research project, your course designers are encouraging you to experience *the limits to certainty* at first hand. They want you to appreciate the immense effort required to advance that certainty by just a whisker. If you do, you will be better qualified to make rational judgements and assess new developments. Then your degree will really mark you out as the wise person it professes you to be.

2. Practicality

Your university teachers can only teach you so much. They are specialists who also have a broad view of their chosen field. They want to infect you with their enthusiasm for their subject but realize that it takes a lifetime to grasp just a fraction of it. So instead of cramming you with ever more dry and ill-remembered knowledge, your lecturers will lead you just far enough down the path of enlightenment to let you strike off on your own. They wish to instil in you the capacity for analytical and critical thinking. They want you to develop your own independence. Your project is one (brilliantly effective) way for you to ease your hand from their reassuring grasp and explore by yourself.

3. Exploitation

Believe it or not, you are about to be exploited. Until now the only person to have gained from your education is you. Now it's time to start the (intellectual) repayments. Your supervisor will want value for the effort he or she puts in: if a piece of research is worth doing, it's worth getting someone to do it and to do it properly.

It is quite likely, for example, that you will find yourself working as part of an existing research team. Your project might be a pilot study, testing a new idea for soundness before major resources are committed. Or you might be slotted into a well-oiled research machine and asked to generate the next set of results. Alternatively, you might be tidying up a loose end in a larger project, or even following up work started by a previous student.

In such circumstances, you will be forced to balance your desire to do your own thing and gain ownership of the subject with the responsibilities of being part of a group effort.

4. Hedonism

For most people, given conducive circumstances, research is enjoyable. The pleasure takes many different forms, sometimes describable in phrases such as: 'The fun of the chase', 'A chance to be really creative', 'A chance to work independently', or 'A release from the formalities of conventional learning'.

The good times may be interspersed with significant periods of frustration, tedium, extreme discomfort or intense dislike, but in the end the positive feelings usually prevail. Many people involved in 'pure' research would argue that the pleasure alone provides them with sufficient reason to continue. Other researchers will pinpoint more externally-important motives, although few would carry on if they really hated it.

Students usually need a strong incentive to embark on something so alien, risky and unpredictable as research for the first time. Surprising as it may seem, staff like giving students pleasant things to do and are social hedonists at heart. Who knows?: you might end up enjoying your research project more than you expect.

▮ WHAT CAN I GET OUT OF IT?

You can benefit in at least six different ways from your project. The balance of benefits will depend on circumstances, but you should experience all of them. Whether your interests eventually overlap with those of your teachers remains to be seen (see Figure 2.1).

1. Ownership

The work you are about to do will be yours and you will have responsibility for it. Whatever you find out will be your contribution to the sum of human knowledge, and those who later make use of that knowledge will have implicit trust in your integrity. That's not just trusting you not to have cheated — it's trusting that you were thorough, that you paid sufficient attention to detail and that the answer you arrived at was based on an objective assessment of the evidence. (Such responsibilities sound frightening but turn out to be really quite straightforward.) Owning the outcome in this way probably makes your project the most self-determining piece of work you have ever done. No one has ever done it before and no one could have safely predicted the outcome (if they had or could, the research would not be worth doing!).

2.   Knowledge and understanding

By the time you have finished your project you may well know as much or more about the subject you have been researching than anyone else *in the entire world*. OK, so you may not, after just a few weeks' work, be able to construct a new theory of evolution or say for certain who really wrote Shakespeare's plays, but your knowledge of genetic selection or textual analysis will be profound. You probably covered these things as standard items in earlier modules, but now you will really start to study them in depth and to understand them in a practical and comprehensive sense. Research is like that: you start to focus on something that seems small and relatively insignificant and in no time at all the material has insidiously entered your head and turned itself into an obsession. It's a bit like putting creosote on a garden fence: it soaks in, forms a reassuringly protective layer and changes the view forever. Suddenly, isolated facts that you learned a long time ago start to assume their rightful place in the scheme of things. Instead of trying to catch up with what others have found, you find you are up to speed and able to lead the expedition from the front. Your theory of evolution may be a lot worse than Darwin's, but at least you now know why. And suddenly you find yourself arguing with new confidence that, after all, Shakespeare probably did write those plays.

3.   Publication

Research results only have value if they are published in some way. A hidden discovery is no discovery at all. Fermat's last theorem had to be re-proven 350 years after his death because the eponymous mathematician himself forgot, deliberately or otherwise, to tell the world how he had worked it out (Singh, 1997); and we will *never* know whether the modern solution is the same as the one referred to by Fermat in his oblique margin note. So, in one way or another, you're going to have to tell the world about what you have done. Remember also that universities are a 'writing culture' – academia revolves around the written word and the transmission of information in an 'objective' format (Popper, 1972). Publication takes different forms. It is not unheard of for the results of undergraduate research to be published as a full refereed paper. More frequently, the work contributes a small but significant amount to work published by the departmental group, with the student's name appearing in the list of authors. These are rare successes. Most commonly the work is written up as a dissertation which, after the initial personal excitement and self-satisfaction have faded, is left to gather dust on departmental or library shelves. That, too, is success. It is the objectification of knowledge, the opening up of private, subjective discovery to the critical but curious eye of the world. At a personal level, your own copy of the dissertation will find a secure home on your bookshelf and will remain a source of pride. As the years go by, the pride may become diluted with cynicism or even embarrassment and you may even wonder why you ever thought it a worthy piece of work. But it is your name in print, your mark on the world. And it is your academic rite of passage.

4. Tangible outcome

Some university disciplines, especially 'applied' subjects such as engineering, architecture, computer science, etc., base projects around the development of a product, a construction or some other tangible outcome. Here the principal end point is not the written dissertation but the creation itself. The object (a machine, a structure, a plan, a computer program, a design) is judged by its ability to perform effectively in the task for which it was conceived. In other words, the outcome delivers its own assessment. The way in which the solution to the problem was arrived at, though interesting, may be less important than the effectiveness of the solution itself. In this case you might also eventually come to view the product as small or insignificant, especially if your career takes you into an industry where productive things happen on a large scale. But, again, don't ever underestimate the value of having cut your teeth within the safe and self-motivated context of student work. What better place is there to find out what personal endeavour and success feel like? How better to experience the process of invention and discovery? This is your opportunity to see a project through from beginning to end and to stamp your own personality on the outcome.

5. Personal development

Carrying out your project will have a profound effect on your personality. You cannot go through all the emotions (excitement, boredom, optimism, despondency, control, desperation, enthusiasm, rejection and more) of research without emerging as a different person. To complete your project, you will need to work harder than ever before and call on personal resources which you never knew you possessed. You will find it necessary to review your outlook, dump some long-held attitudes and beliefs and adopt new ones. Some of the changes in you will affect others, particularly your close friends and family, and may do so in ways which you find unexpected or even undesirable. Research has its own personal characteristics and emotional associations. Recognize them when you can and turn them to advantage.

6. Job value and skills

Employers are impressed by research work. It's a safe bet that when you eventually get called for a job interview and they scan your CV, the project is the item they'll be most interested in. They will want to find out not how much you *know* but how much you are capable of *achieving*. Anyone can follow a syllabus and pass exams but a project requires a unique individual effort. They will want to know about your project because it will be the thing that makes you different. They will also want to know about the skills you have gained. Any interesting job or career involves, by definition, being confronted by new challenges. An experience may be new and unpredicted, but having a sound personal skill-base ensures that you approach it with courage and confidence. Projects are a brilliant source of skills.

■ NOVELTY AND OWNERSHIP

How 'new' or 'original' does your research have to be? In some cases, it may be hard to locate the element of originality in the work you are about to undertake. Many university dissertations are not 'novel' in the strict sense but involve reviewing the literature or surveying some other form of existing information. Such studies may appear to have less intrinsic value than work which generates totally new data or results, but this is emphatically *not* the case. However many times the field has been studied before, *your* view of it will be new and unique. Knowledge and understanding are subjective – they depend on the observer and do not exist without the observer being there. Your task is to take that information, give it life and wring as much value from it as possible. You will find new connections, unpredictable shapes and unforeseen implications. In so doing, it will become yours.

A CLOSER LOOK AT SKILLS

Completing your project successfully and being pleased with the outcome requires you to exercise a number of skills. You possess many of these already (questioning, listening, analysing, summarizing, writing, organizing, meeting deadlines, etc.), either because they are commonplace 'life skills' or because they result from your educational experiences. Other skills will need to be developed as you go. No one expects you to be a brilliant exponent of all, or any, of the skills you need right from the outset – you will develop and enhance them as the project progresses.

Some of the skills you possess, and some of those you will gain by carrying out your project, are directly related to your subject area and part of the knowledge-base you acquire during study ('subject-specific skills'). Others are common to many different kinds of project and more adaptable to new situations. Even if your course is vocational, or if you decide on a career in research, your existing subject-specific abilities will not be useful indefinitely – you will constantly find yourself having to retrain to keep up to speed. It is the adaptable skills which will have lasting value (Box 2.1). Skills exist on a 'use it or lose it' basis: they need to be nurtured. The ability to learn, develop and improve is itself a highly adaptable and long-lasting skill.

Adaptable skills are all *highly context sensitive*. In other words, the way you learn them, your degree of competency and your ability to exploit them depend on the situations in which they are gained and used. It is not realistic simply to check your skills off against a list or to scale an abstract ladder of achievement levels. To see what this means, consider a football player and a basketball player: although both may spend a great deal of time developing 'ball skills' and can achieve national or international levels of ability, the nature of their skills remain different. It would be difficult to compare their abilities in absolute terms (are they good at shooting, dribbling, passing, etc?). Nevertheless, a footballer learning to play basketball (or vice versa) might be expected to pick up the new skills quite rapidly, not because of inherent physical fitness or quick reactions, but because of a profound and adaptable understanding of how a ball behaves.

TYPES OF SKILLS

Adaptable skills can be divided into four groups as shown in Table 2.2 All of these are available from project work of one kind or another. The lists are not exhaustive or restrictive and are intended to be flexible.

Box 2.1   Adaptable skills

The characteristic which people who work in familiar and unfamiliar contexts have in common is not their knowledge but their skills and abilities. Adaptable skills (sometimes called 'transferable skills') are skills that you gain in one situation but can apply in another.

In the following diagram, possession of a suitably adaptable skill enables you to move with confidence from position A to position D, as well as to B and C:

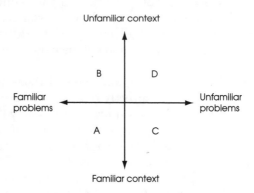

It is essential to realize, however, that the process of adaptation is not always straightforward. Skills are only effective *in context* and it will probably take some effort and determination to adapt to the new situation. You might also find that the skill only becomes fully exploitable once you have acquired some additional knowledge related to the new task or endeavour.

But what about the knowledge gained as a student? Won't that be useful once university is past? Some of it will, for sure, but you won't be able to rely on it. Its own context will change and it may become dated or even obsolete.

What you need to take with you from university is a range of adaptable skills which you can call on at any time:

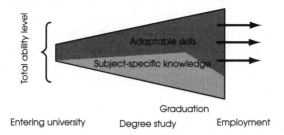

The knowledge gained from your project may be of surprisingly limited value after the work is completed but the skills you have gained have the potential to be useful to you for a long, long time.

You will not acquire all the skills but you should gain some from each column. The lists can be added to, rearranged or regrouped in any way that you feel is more appropriate to what you are doing. Your supervisor or tutor might also have some views on what is listed.

Process skills

These are things you need to be able to do to make progress in your chosen subject. They are not specific to your project alone, although in practice they do comprise a continuum from the very general to the highly distinctive and specific. They are the trademark skills of your discipline area (law, biology, sociology, art and design, engineering, etc.) and help to mark you out as a graduate of that discipline. Many of them apply to all disciplines. The earlier modules in your course will probably have prepared you for some of them or at least raised your awareness of the processes involved. Your project may well be the first opportunity you have for demonstrating what you have acquired. Unless you plan a complete change of direction after graduation, you will need many of these skills for a long time to come.

Table 2.2 Types of adaptable skill obtainable from research project work			
Process skills	*Presentation skills*	*Management skills*	*Personal skills*
Problem formulation	Language skills	Project planning	Independence
Problem-solving	Data presentation	Setting objectives	Self-confidence
Assessing information	Oral communication	Project management	Self-reliance
Sifting evidence	Audience awareness	Progress review	Self-discipline
Research techniques	Debating and arguing	Time management	Self-enquiry
Library searching	Persuading and encouraging	Working to deadlines	Imagination
Use of literature	Using display technology	Working with others	Originality
Developing arguments	Report writing	Person management	Ability to learn
Designing experiments	Word-processing	Coping with crises	Adaptability
Data analysis	Desk-top publishing	Entrepreneurship	Acceptance of criticism
Attention to detail			
Numeracy			
Literacy			
Computing skills			
Laboratory skills			
Safety awareness			

Presentational skills

During the course of your project you will need to present your work to others in several different ways. This requires that you can:

- write clearly and concisely;
- use terminology appropriate to the subject and audience;
- use your voice to best advantage;
- illustrate what you have to say;
- use presentational equipment (slides, computers, OHP, sound systems, etc.) confidently;
- capture and hold your audience's attention;
- present and defend a reasoned argument.

Doing these things effectively takes practice. Few of us are naturally gifted at any of them. By learning some of these skills, you will be turning yourself into a professional communicator. Unless you plan a long-term career in supermarket shelf replenishment or two-wheel fast-food delivery, these skills will be needed for the rest of your working life. Gain them when you can, improve them as you use them, be proud of them, and exploit them at every opportunity.

Management skills

These are the skills you need to be professional. They enable you to get the job done productively and efficiently, to work as part of a team and to get satisfaction from whatever you are doing. The basic skills of management are best acquired by experience (including training courses if appropriate), by exposure to new challenges, by observing others and by open-minded reflection on what has passed.

Books on management skills are available in large quantities at airport bookstalls but are generally aimed at the business community. They should only be purchased if you are embarking on an extremely long flight and all the decent novels are sold out; and then only read if you have seen the in-flight movie twice already. At this stage in your career you need to be most concerned with managing your own work effectively, being productive and adapting to the needs of the group.

Personal skills

These are the most difficult skills to define, recognize and measure, but are none the less real for all that. They sometimes creep up on you unnoticed but it is possible, and never too late, to develop them consciously. It helps if you can take a step back at intervals and work out which ones you already possess, which ones need refreshing and which have passed you by. Whether or not you possess particular personal skills can sometimes be determined most easily by someone else; you may be fortunate enough to have an honest and objective friend with whom you can make an appraisal of these skills from time to time.

GAINING SKILLS

This book recognizes the enormous potential of research project work as a source of adaptable skills and encourages you to consolidate and improve your abilities at every opportunity. Its emphasis is on skill acquisition through *doing*, rather than through *specific learning*. Other parts of your university course may have included specific learning experiences related to skills; you should take advantage of these because they will be beneficial to all aspects of your study and will assist you in obtaining a good job when you graduate.

From this point on there are two approaches to improving your skill level:

1.   Start work on your project and develop the skills you need as you go along.
2.   Get a book on skill development, decide which skills you think you need to improve on, and work through the practical exercises.

This book advocates the first approach. This is because the skill potential of projects is invariably very high and because you probably have little time to embark on a separate programme of personal skill training (why work out on an exercise bike when you could be cycling to work?). To gain advantage, however, you need to be self-aware, self-reliant and self-critical.

One advantage of the second approach is that it provides you with an ordered plan of work and a built-in means of monitoring your progress. Its disadvantage is that the exercises are not always easy to do in context and may not be exactly what you need: they take time and do not *of themselves* contribute anything productive to the work in hand (doing your project or other academic work).

In practice, you might want to choose a combined approach. There are several books specifically devoted to skill development within the context of university study. Drew and Bingham (1997) for example, contains practical advice on several types of study- and work-related skills. It provides graded work sheets and exercises and encourages you to reflect on your levels of achievement. The Bibliography lists many other useful books, including several on the writing skills you will need when you come to write up your dissertation.

■ DEVELOPING SKILLS BY EXPERIENCE

Learning and developing skills by experience is fun. Part of the enjoyment comes from recognizing that you are already a surprisingly skilful individual. Other enjoyment comes from making mistakes, within a relatively secure and supportive environment, and watching improvements occur. However, you will *not* learn or develop a skill simply by:

❑   listening to someone else talk about it (whatever their own level of ability, the depth of their experience, your attentiveness or their experience as a teacher);
❑   thinking about it;
❑   discussing it;
❑   reading about it.

No, what you need to do first and foremost is get out there and get on with it. Once you have recognized a particular skill and begun to practise it you will be able to:

❑   assess for yourself the level of ability you are starting from;
❑   get objective opinions from others about where your strengths and weaknesses lie;
❑   devise a plan for making improvements.

You are entering what is sometimes called an experiential learning cycle. You can enter the cycle at any point, although 'planning' and 'doing' are the best places to begin (see Figure 2.2). In some cases, especially with subject-specific skills and skills of process you might need to seek some practical training or background information in order to get started. The important thing is that you always continue right round the cycle and that you never leave it, at least for as long as the skill continues to be needed.

Figure 2.2   The experiential learning cycle (Kolb, 1984)

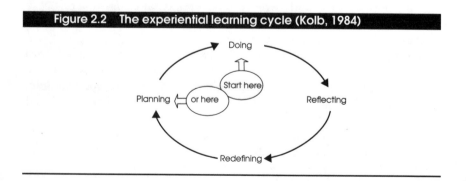

The types of activity involved at each stage are illustrated in Table 2.3. Depending on the nature of the skill, its importance to your work and your own attitude, the reflecting, redefining and planning can be done formally (for example, noted down in a log or diary, or brought into discussions with your supervisor) or just kept in your head. Similarly, the nature of your work will dictate whether your level of ability can be quantified objectively (for example, time taken to translate a foreign text) or not (ability to work independently or as part of a group).

Table 2.3	Components and activities of the experiential learning cycle
Cycle stage	*Type of activity*
Doing	Using the skill Taking calculated risks Completing assignments Carrying out practice runs Attending training courses Working on placement Showing others how to do things
Reflecting	Reviewing results and outcomes Watching a video of your performance Comparing achievements over time Discussing your contribution to the group effort Obtaining feedback from the audience Seeking your supervisor's advice Peer review
Redefining	Watching others use the skill Reading a skill guide Listening to an expert lecture Summarizing general principles Reviewing preconceptions Identifying gaps in knowledge Setting new goals Defining new boundaries
Planning	Preparing for the next occasion Improving resource availability Making changes to procedures Identifying priorities Devising action plans

FITTING IT IN

This chapter looks at managing project time within the context of your other degree studies. Sound **time management** is a precious skill and one which will be particularly valuable to you as you try to balance the different components of your studies. This book is not a manual of time management techniques and this chapter is not bulging with mind games or magic answers. In Chapter 5 we'll consider in more detail how to manage the time and effort you put into the different parts of the project itself, but for now the focus is on time *planning* and your attitude towards it. Happily, improved time management skills will turn out to be an inevitable consequence of carrying out your research project. This is guaranteed.

There is more to effective time planning than just making lists and prioritizing. It has to do with:

- developing self-confidence;
- being reflective, self-aware and self-critical;
- taking a constructive approach to life.

Buy a book on time management if you want to, but the last thing you have time for at this stage is a set of exercises which may not be relevant to your work and by themselves get you no further forward in your project. You will automatically develop an effective battery of time management techniques for yourself provided that you construct the right framework and keep a check on what you are doing. The rest of this chapter is about how to do this.

■ TIME IN THE BALANCE

Time management is a balancing act which has **real** and **virtual** components. Imagine an acrobat on a tightrope. He has two concurrent balancing acts to perform:

> The **real** one – staying on the wire – impresses the crowd and is what he gets paid for. He finds it straightforward because he is skilful and has been doing it everyday since childhood. If he ever falls off, which is rare these days, the safety net saves broken bones.

> The **virtual** one is the one in his head. This is much more threatening since it has to do with confidence and pride. Confidence and pride are fragile, difficult skills to master, even for someone with his long experience. It takes courage to step out on the wire each night: will this be the time when he lets his audience and himself down? He is a perfectionist and the danger he faces seems immense, even if the physical risk is small. To be successful he needs, above all things, a balanced and relaxed mind.

In balancing your time, you have choices to make. At one extreme, you could plan to do very few things, have a good time, always stay well within your known capabilities and end up with an ordinary but uninspiring piece of work. At the other, you could try to do everything, do it all perfectly, never take a break and drive yourself insane in the process. The first option is the tightrope walker inching slowly along a short, low rope: no chance of falling off but uninteresting to watch. The second option is the walker attempting something new and spectacular on the highwire each night but not taking time out to practise or put a proper display programme together: the audience is impressed by the danger but upset by the falls and disappointed by the show.

Or you could steer a middle course: do the right amount of work, do it properly rather than perfectly, extend your capabilities by taking a few calculated risks, achieve more than you might have expected and yet remain sociable, stable and generally in control of yourself. But how do you know what the right amount of work is? How do you give your work structure and organization? And how can you stretch yourself effectively while at the same time allowing the rest of your life retain some semblance of normality?

A PRACTICAL STRATEGY

Try using these three components as the basis for your time management strategy:

1   Work smarter, not harder (Table 3.1) .
2.   Create a framework (Box 3.1).
3.   Review and reflect (Box 3.2).

Once a strategy has been established, you will find it easier to incorporate the detailed elements of time management associated with the day-to-day running of your project (see Chapter 7).

Table 3.1 Working smarter, not harder (or 'How to do less well, not more badly')	
Working harder	*Working smarter*
Using more hours	Using existing hours more effectively
Getting up earlier, going to bed later or not at all	Setting a work plan for the day
Scheduling things on scraps of paper	Scheduling things in a diary
Rushing meals; missing meals	Including meal times in your daily plan
Doing one thing at a time, perfectly	Doing things with a purpose
Doing everything, all at once	Doing several things properly
Reading nothing, photocopying everything	Reading judiciously, accurately and once
Repeatedly reorganizing information	Organizing information effectively
Gathering information just in case it is needed	Taking complete and effective notes
Gathering data before knowing what to do with it	Having a clear strategy for data analysis
Pushing on regardless	Getting help before it is needed
Looking after everything and everyone, all the time	Delegating some less personal responsibilities
Putting hard jobs aside in favour of easy ones	Anticipating outcomes; having a fall-back position
Filling the diary with back-to-back meetings	Preparing for meetings and focusing on outcomes
Re-reading post and answering it later	Handling post once
Doing other people's work instead of your own	Improving your own understanding by helping others
Pushing ahead without a break	Reflecting on the day's achievements

Box 3.1   Creating a framework

Your project is not the only thing you have to do and, if you are to obtain a good degree, it is essential that you maintain the right balance between the project and other work. Overall, you probably know roughly how much effort you need to put into each taught module because their demands and rates of progress are familiar to you. The project module is unfamiliar and the chances are that you are about to climb a steep learning curve. This simple framework will help to prevent you from getting distracted and spending disproportionate amounts of time on the work piling up ahead.

Modularized courses and credit ratings make it easy to work out the proportion of marks allocated to each part of the course. Course designers work to an explicit relationship between credits and expected hours of work (teaching, contact and private study time).

Once you know what this relationship is (ask your personal tutor if you don't), do a rough calculation to translate the relative credit rating of your project into hours or days of the working week.

❏   Start by calculating the amount of time you should be spending on your project. Base your calculation on the relative mark allocation for your project or its credit weighting.
❏   Draw up a timetable and set aside a day, or half day, or 12h per week (or whatever you have calculated) for *work* on the project. Vary the proportions for different parts of the semester or particular parts of the year if that is appropriate in the context of your course and other things you know you will have to do.
❏   *Set out on your project with these calculations clearly in mind and stick to them as far as possible.*

You already know how your course performance so far reflects your strengths and weaknesses in various subjects and various types of study. As a result, you are already highly skilled at adjusting your effort to iron out some of the uneven areas.

The trouble is, of course, that it is not quite so easy as that. Knowing, for example, that on a credit basis you should be spending one day each week on your project and four on other modules is all very well, but you know it won't turn out that way. For one thing, your other course work may be unevenly distributed over the semester, perhaps demanding periods of intense essay or practical report writing interspersed with relatively slacker times. On the other hand, your project may turn out to include periods of wall-to-wall practical work when the best you can hope for other modules is a frantic dash between lectures and tutorials.

It is quite realistic to expect academic life to be like that. What you have to do is to try as far as possible to balance the **sum** of the effort in each direction. This is the only way to get a good degree, representative of your abilities.

Once you have started to think about your project, try the following as a means of keeping track of what you are doing:

☐   Keep a diary and check it frequently
-    **Include** everything to do with your project (talking to supervisor, scanning the literature, writing a research plan, learning techniques, chasing obscure references); but
-    **Exclude** thinking time: this is impossible to measure (unless you are highly skilled in Zen!). Your enthusiasm and motivation will dictate how it is allocated.
☐   After a few weeks, reflect on how the balance looks. Take into account any unavoidable clusters of deadlines and any special difficulties you have encountered.
☐   Review your tactics and make adjustments aimed at bringing the work back to equilibrium.
☐   Now, try to look ahead and anticipate deadlines and periods of intensity to come.

Remember that time spent actually **working** (listening, discussing, reading, writing, etc.) on a subject does not always correlate with the time spent **thinking** about it. You are studying for a degree not running a car factory – there is no simple equation relating energy in and product out.

The key process going on here is **reflection**: stepping back for a moment or two and looking, as dispassionately as possible, at how things are shaping. What you are *really* doing is recognizing what self-motivated work entails; you are working out how to make your time and effort as productive as possible when the rules are left up to you. You can fully expect to get so wrapped up in your research that you would happily spend all your time on it. It's up to you to spot when that happens and accommodate it. Maintain the balance and stay on the rope.

Ideally, try to establish this kind of reflective activity as part of your work routine, and continue it through your studies.

THE MIRACULOUS TIME CAKE

The economic metaphor of 'dividing the cake' is a handy one (see Figure 3.1). There are only so many productive hours in the day and you have many calls on your time. Good, solid, academic work is what you should be doing, but sometimes it seems that there are so many other things to do that the work can easily get left out. There are only so many useful days in the semester, and vacations have their own financial imperatives. The time cake is limited and its slices must be carefully rationed.

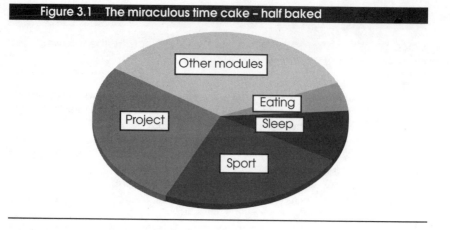

Figure 3.1   The miraculous time cake – half baked

So, given that your time is full already, how are you going to find the additional space to do a good project? Well, here's the miracle. If you apply an effective work strategy, your time cake will *spontaneously* increase in size (see Figure 3.2). Its diameter will not change, but its depth will increase noticeably. Each slice will be taller and contain more fruit. In other words, you will get more productive work done in the same amount of time.

These are the sorts of things you might notice:

❏   Calculations that once took all morning will be finished before coffee time.

❏   A research paper that might once have demanded a whole evening of beer-free concentration, will be read and assimilated in less time than it takes to photocopy its abstract.

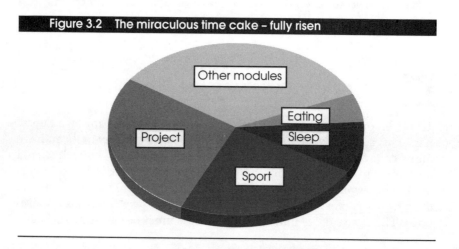

Figure 3.2   The miraculous time cake – fully risen

☐   A meeting that might once have drifted on all afternoon without really reaching a conclusion will achieve its objective in half an hour allowing everyone to leave knowing exactly what they have to do.

☐   Two-page progress reports will be written up, spell-checked and printed without having to destroy promising social relationships.

Your work will be more efficient and you will pack more into each hour and each day than you ever thought possible. A kind of reverse Parkinson's Law applies:

> The more items of work there are to complete in a given period, the less time each of them takes.

alternatively expressed in the management aphorism:

> If you want to get something done, ask a busy person to do it.

And the other curious thing is that these speedily completed items lose nothing in quality. In fact, they are sharper, better focused, of greater use and more easily remembered than the ponderous, struggle-filled efforts of earlier times.

STAGE

2

PLANNING IT

CHOOSING A TOPIC

To make a success of your project, there are some questions you need to ask right from the start. You will have been thinking or wondering about your project for some time, possibly even for several semesters. Now is the time to start informing yourself about what project work entails and to try to discover what will be expected of you.

DEPARTMENTAL STRATEGIES

University departments adopt a number of different approaches to the inclusion of project work in the degree course. The following are some of the more common ones and you will soon find out which applies to you.

1. Free/Optional
The department leaves it up to you to express an interest in doing a piece of research, perhaps as an optional part of another module. After locating a suitable supervisor, you work out a set of objectives and agree on a mutually acceptable format for the finished product. It is up to you to find the time to do the work within the framework of the rest of your course.

2. Regulated
The project is an obligatory part of the degree course, often forming an identifiable, credit-rated module. At an appropriate time, the department prompts you to decide on a topic and sets aside designated course time for the completion of the work. You are given clear information on the type of work that is expected of you. A set of regulations describes the format of the dissertation and you are given deadlines for the completion of interim reports and the final dissertation or other outcome.

3. Highly structured
Under this approach, you follow a series of research modules culminating in the completion of the project. The modules may include group sessions on experimental design and analysis which are completed as coursework assignments. You may have to carry out a feasibility study or submit plans and proposals for preliminary evaluation. You may also be required to cost the project. In some cases, the course of modules may extend from earlier semesters of the degree.

4. Additional time
A number of university departments rate the need for undergraduates to experience research so highly that they add a supplementary period of time, often a whole academic year, to the degree course. The project is the major, perhaps only, element in the year although it may be backed up with training in research methods. The extra provision may be limited to students achieving a certain grade in their other studies. Sometimes it amounts to an extra degree and may be used, for example, to turn a Bachelor's degree into a Master's degree.

 ## CHOOSING THE SUBJECT

Many of the questions you'll want to ask at this stage have to do with deciding on the topic of the study. How much choice you have in this will depend on departmental policy. In general, there are three possibilities:

1. Hobson's choice
It is rare for departments to allocate projects without some allowance for student decision-making, but it does happen. You must accede to departmental policy, but this does not mean that the staff are unapproachable or unavailable for negotiation. They will appreciate your ideas about how the work might be slanted or adapted. After all, they want you to be interested and successful – supervising a reluctant student is no fun for anyone and very unlikely to be productive.

2. Choosing from a list
Some departments offer their students a list of potential project subjects from which to choose. You may be presented with just a list of titles, or there may be more extensive background information, perhaps even a list of key papers to read. The list may have been carefully designed to spread the supervisory load equally among the staff. If so, you may find that there is little flexibility and that there are popular projects to be fought over. The proposed subjects will reflect the research interests of

the department and may be associated with the ongoing work of academic staff, research staff, postgraduates or previous undergraduate students. After scanning the list, you need to move fast to inform yourself about the best option. Some criteria on which to base your choice are given in Box 4.1. Whatever happens, don't be passive at this stage. Go and talk to the staff involved. Negotiate with your colleagues. You were offered a choice, so be assertive and don't end up with an unwanted or inappropriate project simply for want of a bit of effort.

3.   Your own idea

Being asked to come up with a subject for your research project may either excite you or fill you with dread. You may see it either as a chance to express yourself and realize a dream or as a threat to the limitations of your existing knowledge and imagination. If you are already sure about which parts of your course interest you the most, or if you have focused on an area of relevance to your career aspirations, you may have little difficulty in identifying an appropriate subject for study. On the other hand, you may not have a clue what to do or where to begin looking. Whichever category you fall into, it is important that you choose something that motivates you. Be selfish. Choose a topic and then ask yourself 'Could I become passionate about it?'.

Box 4.2 suggests some ways of identifying a suitable topic. Box 4.3 describes the Mind Mapping® approach to sorting and organizing your ideas. You may find this especially useful if your ideas are vague at present or if you find your thoughts in a muddle and you cannot see an easy, logical way through.

Even if it is departmental policy to offer project titles, you may have thought of a topic which you think needs investigating, perhaps arising out of something you heard at a lecture or seminar, or based on something you have read. This can be very exciting, and will impress your tutors. Talk to them about it and try to push your case. You probably already have a feel for the research interests of staff in your department, and it is more than likely that your attitude to the discipline has already been coloured by their interests. If you come up with an idea which is totally outside their experience, while they may do their best to assist you, you cannot expect them to provide the expert help and advice in the subject which would otherwise be available.

Don't be put off at this stage if you cannot see how to ask the right research questions, let alone carry out the project itself (undergraduates emerging from taught courses rarely have the experience or depth of knowledge needed to do this immediately). It is much more likely that a general area of interest becomes apparent to you and that this

Box 4.1   Deciding which project to do

This is a checklist of criteria to use in deciding which project to choose. If the answer to any item is 'Don't know', inform yourself about it as soon as possible. Talk to the project course leader, the project supervisor or to another member of staff, or do some general reading for yourself.

Criterion	'Yes', 'No', 'Don't know'	Importance and reasoning
Is it within my broad area of interest?		This is crucially important – you must have the right background for the work.
Do I have a specific interest in this topic already?		A pre-existing interest will influence your choice but a 'No' here should not prevent you from choosing this project. There is every chance that you will become interested, even passionate about it.
Do I get on with the supervisor?		Only answer 'No' if the feeling is very strong and based on good evidence. If 'Don't know', assume that you will get on – it's amazing how human academic staff become when you get them on their own, talking about their favourite topic.
Will I be working alone or in a team?		This will not affect your ownership of the topic but may affect your freedom in designing the study and performing the work. Are there clear guidelines about which parts of the work are to be shared and which will be individual contributions?
Are there any additional financial costs?		Any such costs should be minor (limited travel, occasional subsistence, vacation residence, etc.) but make sure you know clearly what they will be and who is going to pay. You will have to pay for the production and duplication of your dissertation.
Do the time demands suit me? Will I have to work out of hours or in vacations?		Be as flexible, accommodating and enthusiastic as you can, but be realistic in recognizing any serious limitations.
What is the skill potential of the project?		This is one of the most important questions to ask. Find out about the subject-related and the adaptable skills you might acquire.

Box 4.2   Sources of ideas for projects

❏   A tv/radio/newspaper item which caught your attention.
❏   Something mentioned in a lecture or tutorial which seemed to be unresolved.
❏   A generalization made by someone outside your field ('Everyone knows that...', 'What's the point of...?', etc.) of which you feel suspicious or which you think could do with testing against the evidence.
❏   Something you have always wondered about.
❏   A hunch you've had for a while.
❏   A quotation that particularly stuck in your mind.
❏   A necessity in need of an invention.
❏   A flick through a current journal.
❏   Previous research projects in the department.
❏   A chat with a postgraduate about their work.
❏   A book or poem you read recently.
❏   An article that caught your eye in the popular journal section of the library.
❏   A public lecture you attended.

Finally, remember that the following are *never* true:

❏   Your idea is inherently worthless.
❏   Your ideas are too way-out, off the wall or intrinsically difficult to study.
❏   Everything is already known.

---

can be honed into shape as a focused research idea through discussions with a member of staff.

To summarize, if you have an idea of your own you should:

1.   inform yourself as fully as possible about recent research on the topic;
2   try hard to sell it to the most approachable or appropriate member of staff, but
3.   not be disappointed if what emerges is rather different from what you originally imagined.

CHOOSING THE *RIGHT* SUBJECT

From this distance, it may seem that choosing the *right* subject (that is, a subject that already interests you deeply), will be crucial in determining whether the project is a success. The choice of subject is certainly important, but not something to get unduly anxious or wound up about.

Box 4.3   Mind Mapping®

You might find this approach helpful for:

- ❐ generating ideas
- ❐ organizing your thoughts
- ❐ solving problems (of memory, concentration, motivation)
- ❐ note-making
- ❐ reflecting on progress
- ❐ planning future work
- ❐ writing up and revising

It is fully described and illustrated in Buzan (1997) *The Mind Map Book*. See also Creme and Lea (1997).

Tony Buzan describes Mind Mapping® as a way of **'radiant thinking'** and suggests that it reflects the radiant architecture of the brain (and other wonders of nature). It is a way of noting your thoughts on paper but, rather than putting facts and ideas down as a list, it encourages you to draw them as a set of relationships. In other words, your thoughts are represented not in an orderly row, like books on a library shelf, but as a network of inter-connected ideas.

Some ideas are central to whole areas of thought while others have more limited links, indicate dead ends, or represent the start of a new way of thinking. As soon as you start to build connections between ideas, other links and interrelationships spring into view. This can be a wonderfully revealing and surprisingly **creative** process.

Mind maps bridge the gap between **thinking** and **writing** and this can make them especially useful in overcoming problems such as writer's block or motivation. The order of ideas in the map is of little importance. Drawing the map therefore encourages you to start somewhere (anywhere). You can revise what you have done as you go along without any of the anxieties of perfection associated with linear lists.

You can use **colours** to link ideas and to make the structure of the map more meaningful to you. And you don't have to use words if words are not your preferred means of expressing yourself; mixtures of pictures, shapes, numbers, and even formulae and musical notation are just as valid if you feel more comfortable with them.

Try using mind maps as a means of **note-making** when you work on the literature for your project. Your notes need to be brief, accurate and effi-cient. They should also reflect your own interpretation of what you have read. These characteristics can be difficult to achieve by means of long-hand text. They are easy to achieve with an uninhibited, graphical approach. The volume of your notes and the time taken to re-read them will be considerably reduced (don't skimp on the formal record of biblio-graphic detail, however).

If you find mind-mapping helpful, you may feel inclined to express your ideas in that way when it comes to **writing up** your thesis. Unfortunately, this is not a generally acceptable format and you will undoubtedly have to adapt to using the more traditional prosaic style. You can, however:

Box 4.3   Continued

❏   use a mind map to arrange your ideas as you work, even if the final form disguises the fact;

❏   include a moderate number of (simple) diagrams to show how the ideas you are discussing are interconnected;

❏   revise for your oral examination using maps you created as you proceeded through your project.

You may find that nothing on the list of topics seems familiar or that, despite your best endeavours, you appear to have ended up with the short straw. The best attitude to take here is that of *constructive optimism*: give it your best shot and all will turn out well.

Most supervisors will tell you that, provided the project is inherently do-able, the pre-existing interests of the student are of minor importance compared with his or her approach to the work. And after completing their projects, most students will tell you (go on, find some and ask them!):

❏   that what they actually did turned out to be quite different from what they had expected at the start, and

❏   that they became totally absorbed in the work and developed new interests, ideas, attitudes and skills in the process.

That's very reassuring and should encourage optimism even if at this stage you don't feel particularly inspired by any of the choices offered. The point is that the *process of research* invariably turns out to be at least as interesting and absorbing as the *subject of the project*.

FIRMING UP THE TITLE

You may need to do a little background reading and hold several meetings with potential supervisors or the project course leader to identify and firm up ideas. Make a start on this yourself but seek advice at the earliest opportunity. The sort of process you might have to go through is illustrated by the examples in Box 4.4. The process of refining the title is really a process of refining the project's content. Thinking about the title will get you thinking about what is feasible. It will make you wonder whether what you want to do has intrinsic value and offers the right amount of scope for your interests and abilities. Don't be too concerned if the title you eventually come up with sounds awkward, over-

Box 4.4   Firming up a project title

Here are two examples of how the scope and title of a project might develop from an initidal idea based on a subject area.

EXAMPLE 1

Subject area   *Cattle diseases*

☐   Step 1   Identify some important cattle diseases; read some general texts.

☐   Step 2   Decide to focus on one: BSE, because this is very topical.

☐   Step 3   Consider possible ways of looking at BSE: origin, related pathologies, aetiology, causative organism, inter-specific transfer, epidemiology, government response, EU attitude, economic cost.

☐   Step 4   Decide to focus on one aspect: epidemiology, because (a) this relates to my career aspirations and (b) the department has experience in this area.

☐   Step 5   Consider possible ranges of study:
-    International, European, national, local, county single herd;
-    throughout history, since start of current epidemic, single year, single month;
-    numerical progression of epidemic, geographical spread of cases.

☐   Step 6   Further reading and discussion with staff member to gauge what is feasible.

Final project title   *A geographical analysis of the occurrence of new BSE cases in Devon cattle herds during 1996.*

Example 2

Subject area   *Public transport policy*

☐   Step 1   Identify some important methods of public transport.

☐   Step 2   Focus on one: rail; based on personal enthusiasm for rail as a way of reducing car usage by commuters.

☐   Step 3   Bright idea: wonder whether the local revivalist steam railway has had any significant effect on transport habits. Should be easy to get information: send a questionnaire to local people.

☐   Step 4   Get basic information: visit railway centre, talk to manager about access to data on passenger numbers.

☐   Step 5   Talk to supervisor: outline the idea, discuss possible approaches, identify some key questions, discuss basics of data collection, questionnaire design and statistical analysis.

Final project title   *An analysis of reactions to the proposed reopening of a local steam railway station amongst people living within a three mile radius.*

specific or even trite. Think of it as provisional at this stage. There will be plenty of time to change it once the aims and objectives of your project begin to take shape. It will also be possible to adjust the title midstream as a result of inevitable changes in research direction as your study proceeds.

 FEASIBILITY STUDY

You may be asked formally to submit an outline project proposal before starting your research. This may be needed for the department to identify the most appropriate supervisor or to enable the resource requirements to be catered for. More importantly as far as you are concerned, the department will consider this initial analysis as part of your initial training in research, so spend quality time on it.

In setting about your feasibility study, you might like to consider how some of the following headings apply to the work you want to do:

- ❐ Time
- ❐ Facilities
- ❐ Access to data
- ❐ Access to methods and techniques
- ❐ Financial resources
- ❐ Certainties, uncertainties and risks
- ❐ Reliance on other people
- ❐ Reliance on events beyond your control
- ❐ Fallback positions

In considering each of these, be as realistic and honest with yourself as possible. Being over ambitious is just as risky as being too cautious. A limited but thoroughly thought-out project plan will get a better reception and be easier to live up to than one which is spectacularly original but poorly founded.

A mark will be awarded for the initial problem identification and analysis; find out what weight this mark carries. Follow any guidelines you are given for the format of this preliminary statement. If little guidance is given, talk to a member of staff about what is needed. At a minimum, you will probably have to provide the following:

- ❐ Title
- ❐ The main question (better still: the hypothesis to be tested)
- ❐ Brief justification and background

- ❐ An outline design
- ❐ An indication of how the information/data is to be collected and analysed
- ❐ A time plan

Some departments also ask for a list of the resources you plan to use and a breakdown of any cost which may be incurred. It would be wise to include such a plan, even if it is not specifically asked for, if only because it will help you to start planning your work.

■ NARROWING THE CHOICE

If you have to choose from a list of projects suggested by staff, there are some important things you will need to find out before making a final decision. As soon as you start to home in on one or two suitable projects, it's time for an in-depth discussion with the supervisor (Box 4.5). The purpose of this discussion is twofold:

- ❐ You need more information (is the project really what you thought it would be from the title?).
- ❐ You need to make sure that the supervisor knows who you are and acknowledges your interest. If the choices become limited and decisions have to be imposed, it will help your case significantly if you have already registered an interest and shown enthusiasm.

Other sources of information:

- ❐ Talk to previous students. Depending on course structure, you may find yourself overlapping with students already working on related material who are nearing completion of their dissertations. Alternatively, there may be recent graduates of the department who are now postgraduate students, research assistants or otherwise still around. Grabbing a few minutes of bar time or sharing a pizza with one or two of them will generate more useful gossip, tips and strategies for handling the supervisor than you ever imagined possible.
- ❐ Look closely at some recently completed dissertations. This is the best way of getting a vision of the task ahead of you. The supervisor may have some or there may be some in a departmental store. These can be valuable even if they are on subjects unrelated to the one you are considering. Take particular note of the following features:

Box 4.5   Choosing the topic: seven key items for discussion with the supervisor

1. Get the supervisor to spend a few minutes describing **the project** to you. Ask questions about anything you don't understand. As well as becoming better informed, you will start to develop a rapport. This will be invaluable, especially if your previous contact with him or her has been distant or limited to formal (lecture) situations.

2. Ask for a clear statement of **the object** of the research. Does the project have a clear goal? You will be working at the edge of existing knowledge but how clear is the edge? Is the edge illuminated by a searchlight or marked by a 'Don't fall off' notice?

3. Find out **why** the project has not been done before and why its time has now come.

4. Find out if **methods** for the work exist or whether you will be expected to develop them as part of the work. Are you guaranteed to obtain results or are there methodological uncertainties.

5. Get an outline **time-scale** for the work. How much background reading will be required? Will you be expected to get on with practical work immediately and catch up on the reading later? Can you expect to have a reasonable amount of time for writing up or will the practical work have to be taken to the wire?

6. What is the likely **outcome**, in addition to the dissertation? Might it be published? Is the work part of an existing group effort? Will your contribution be properly recognized?

7. What **skills** might you reasonably expect to acquire by doing the project? If you have a specific career in mind, ask what value these skills and the specific content of the project might have.

(a) Length, arrangement of sections and numbering
(b) Presentation of data and diagrams
(c) Use and content of appendices
(d) Citation systems
(e) Method of binding

You will be given formal guidance on these matters later on but it is still useful to see how they apply in practice and the degree of latitude accepted by the department.

Be critical rather than passive at this stage – the existing dissertations will not all have been produced to the high standard that you will set for yours. Some of the examples you look at may suggest ways of **not** doing things. Ask the supervisor to point you towards a couple of examples, perhaps one good and one not so good. Find out what mark they were given. Ask for guidance if you don't understand why something has been done in a particular way or why one dissertation scored better than another.

▪ MAKING THE CHOICE

☐   NOW make your choice and stick with it
  – No regrets
  – No envy of others
  – No second thoughts
☐   NOW is the time to burn some energy
  – to get enthusiastic
  – to get totally absorbed
  – and to show everyone that you made the right choice

CHAPTER

5

PLANNING YOUR RESEARCH

FRAMING THE QUESTION

Once you have decided on your project topic and obtained all the preliminary advice you need, the next important task is to define the question you are asking. You will need to get your supervisor's advice on this but you should make a start yourself. Table 5.1 describes some types of approach you might take and the key question to ask in each case.

Table 5.1 Framing the question	
Approach	*Key question*
Set an hypothesis and obtain data to test it	Is it true that ...?
Measure something which has not been measured before	What is the size of ...?
Find out how something works/why something happens	What is the cause of ...?
Model a possible event	What would happen if ...?
Sole a practical problem	How can ... be achieved?
Create a useful product or practical solution	How can ... be done, or done better?
Investigate an historical event	When and why did it happen?
Investigate an historical character	Who caused it to happen?
Investigate a significant place	Where did it happen? Why did it happen here?
Test public opinion	What do people think about ...?
Study a process or policy	What is the mechanism of ... and how can it be improved or made more efficient?

Statements of approach can be as varied as the subject demands. They may be clear statements of intent or just general expressions of interest. Key questions, on the other hand, give concrete shape and form to your intention. They start with a limited range of words, as indicated below:

- ❏ What?
- ❏ Why?
- ❏ When?
- ❏ How?
- ❏ Where?
- ❏ Who?

Get a piece of paper and start scribbling out a list which identifies the approach and key questions in the manner shown above. The first list will be a bit of a mess, so have several goes at it. When you have something coherent, make a readable copy and go and talk to your supervisor about what you have come up with. Note that at this stage the list says nothing about the methodology you will use – this a list of ideas, concepts and questions. Its aim is to focus your thoughts so that when you do come to plan your work you have a clear idea of what you are trying to do and why you are doing it.

■ SETTING A WORKING HYPOTHESIS

In the pure and applied sciences, research work usually starts with an hypothesis. In other fields, the word 'hypothesis' may not be used but the research invariably starts with an idea, a question, a conjecture or some kind of supposition however flimsy. Even where the research appears to be predominantly descriptive, it can be surprisingly instructive to try to reformulate the study in terms of 'hypothesis testing'. It is likely that research work in most fields, with the possible exceptions of 'creative' and 'action' research, could be approached in this manner even though it may not be usual to do so.

The hypothesis is a useful means of identifying the right question, of setting clear and coherent goals and for working out how and when a reliable answer will be obtained. To use this approach effectively, it is necessary to be quite clear about what an hypothesis is and what it is not.

An hypothesis is (after *Chambers English Dictionary*, 1990):

- ❏ a supposition;
- ❏ a proposition assumed for the sake of argument;
- ❏ a theory to be made more probable (or proved[*]) or disproved by reference to observations (or logical deduction[*]); ([*]in mathematics. See Singh, 1997)
- ❏ a provisional explanation for something;
- ❏ only useful if it is capable of being wrong.

An hypothesis is not:

- ❏ reliable;
- ❏ self-evident;
- ❏ certain;
- ❏ inevitably correct;
- ❏ the last word;
- ❏ the complete explanation;
- ❏ the only explanation.

The hypothesis should be written as a statement which is as simple and unambiguous as you are currently able to make it. It may be a single, short sentence or a group of sentences which make positive general statements such as:

- ❏ P is caused by . . .
- ❏ Q depends on . . .
- ❏ R only happens under conditions of . . .
- ❏ The rate of change of S is proportional to . . .
- ❏ Most people believe that . . .

When setting up a working hypothesis, ask yourself the following questions:

1. Is it testable (can it be falsified, could it be wrong)?
2. Is it the simplest explanation consistent with all the known facts?
3. Is it appropriate to the context?
4. Does it move from the specific (the instance you are investigating) to the general (all possible instances of the phenomenon)?

The answer to all of these should be 'Yes'. If any of your answers is 'No' or 'Not sure', you have some more thinking to do.
    You should also ask the following questions:

5. Is it the only possible explanation consistent with all the known facts? (Think of as many alternative hypotheses, consistent with points 1–3 in the list above, as possible).

6.   Does it imply a causal relationship which can be justified by the evidence available? (Correlations may suggest, but do not prove, causality.)

■ CHARTING A COURSE

The outcome of your research is unknown at this early stage. Making firm plans for any kind of travel can be difficult when you don't know quite where you want to go or how long each leg of the journey will take. What you can do from the start, however, is set a sensible strategic course. That way, as well as learning by your mistakes and wrong turnings, you will avoid catastrophes and maintain momentum.

Discussions with your supervisor will have focused your attention on the detail of the project and on the main questions to be addressed. You will have a good idea of the approach you want to take and where to start. You will also know how much time there is to complete the work and have started to draw up a preliminary timetable of events.

The principal steps in the design and execution of a research project are summarized in Box 5.1. This model is based on the principle of *hypothesis testing* as it is applied in the natural sciences and shows that knowledge advances not by improving certainty but by reducing uncertainty.

(*Note:* If you find the idea of an hypothesis, or of hypothesis testing, completely meaningless within the context of your discipline, or if you find yourself struggling to make sense of your research topic in these terms, you might want to ignore some of the advice in this section. Be sure, nevertheless, that you are able to make a clear formulation of the purpose of your project and satisfy yourself that its outcome will be intellectually and academically rigorous.)

Box 5.1   Steps in research project design and execution (adapted from Martin and Bateson, 1993)

This list shows the sequence of intellectual and practical events which takes place in research, particularly in the pure and applied sciences.

The sequence is circular: it begins with a question and hypothesis and ends, not with an answer, but with further questions and hypotheses. Progress is made by excluding incorrect hypotheses and refining the question.

1.   Formulate initial question and make preliminary observations.
    –   Questions may come from previous knowledge, published information or previous observations. They may be broad or specific.

Box 5.1   Continued

2.   Formulate hypotheses and make predictions.
   - Make a range of reasonable hypotheses based on existing knowledge. Be as imaginative as possible.
   - Read the relevant literature in depth, being as selective and focused as possible.
   - Make specific, testable predictions.

3.   Design a strategy and choose methods.
   - Focus on the key questions and consider ways of approaching them.
   - Define the variables to be measured, as narrowly and clearly as possible.
   - Choose methods which are practical and which will most clearly distinguish between competing hypotheses.
   - Determine the number of observations* needed.
   - Imagine the shape the data* will have and decide how it will be analyzed.

4.   Practise and validate methods.
   - Learn methods, creating and adapting as necessary.
   - Determine the reliability (accuracy, precision, specificity, sensitivity) of the methods, rejecting any that are insufficiently reliable.
   - Review the number of observations needed, based on reliability criteria.

5.   Collect data.
   - Obtain the data using the methods specified. Use the same methods throughout.
   - Collect only the amount of data needed to answer the question.

6.   Analyse data.
   - Do simple analyses and obtain summary statistics.*
   - Investigate apparently important results with more complex statistics, but keep the analysis as simple as possible.
   - Don't draw more conclusions than the data will support.
   - Distinguish between generating new hypotheses from the data and testing them.

7.   Test initial hypotheses.
   - Return to the initial hypotheses. Delete those which your data show to be no longer valid. Whatever remains, remains valid.

8.   Draw conclusions and make new hypotheses.
   - Reconsider the wider questions which you started out with in the light of the revised set of hypotheses.
   - Reconsider the published literature and other information.

9.   Make new hypotheses and think of strategies to test them.

*The meaning of 'observation' and 'data' and the importance of statistics will depend on the nature of the research and the subject area.

Box 5.2   A two-stage approach to project time allocation – Stage 1

Stage 1

Anticipate that, over the length of time available, the work will divide itself neatly and sequentially into three equal parts: **planning, doing** and **writing up**. (See Table 5.2 for the activities which make up each part.)

These parts are discrete and there is a logical progression from one to the next:

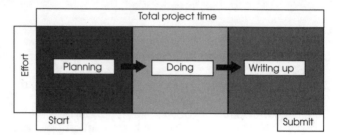

Follow this scheme and your project will be firmly grounded on careful planning. The research work will begin and end at predictable times, allowing you to spread your data collection and follow it up with careful and rigorous analysis. Finally, the results will be written up at a measured pace and the dissertation will be printed and bound in good time for submission.

Wouldn't this be great? After all, is it not how research papers and dissertations *represent* the logical and relentless flow of academic progress ('Introduction, Materials and Methods, Results, Discussion')?

Sorry, but this is fiction. No project ever turned out this way. It is too idealistic and completely unworkable.

Imagine the effect of the following:

☐   your work is governed by seasonal imperatives (for example, biological cycles, climate, the sociological calendar, etc.) and you have no choice but to start *doing* long before the *planning* is complete;

☐   you are obliged to *write* an interim report for a sponsor when you have only just started *doing*;

☐   your other degree work is unevenly spread and you suddenly have to let the project lapse in favour of essays that need completing;

☐   the project involves a crucial field trip that takes you away from the library for several weeks just when you were getting to grips with the literature;

☐   after a few weeks of *doing* you suddenly need more background information and your supervisor decides on a better experimental design;

☐   the survey data you collected after such careful planning turns out to have greater than anticipated variance and you suddenly find yourself needing to recruit more interviewees;

☐   the analytical method you were going to depend on is less robust than you expected and the analysis takes four weeks instead of two;

☐   that halfway through *writing up* you find another crucial experiment that needs *doing*.

It is not difficult to think of a hundred reasons why the parts of the project are no longer as neatly arranged as you might have hoped. You won't be far into **Stage 1** before the parts start to overlap and your idealistic notions of perfect time management lie torn and crumpled in the wastepaper basket.

You have no choice: abandon **Stage 1**, and move to **Stage 2** . . . (Box 5.3).

Box 5.3   A two-stage approach to project time allocation – Stage 2

Stage 2

Having abandoned Stage 1 as unworkable, your project looks as if it is going to turn out more like this:

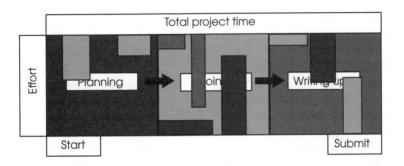

The underlying order seems to remain but you are forced to do things out of turn, to turn back, to anticipate. Sometimes several things need doing at once. At other times you have to do work you are unprepared for. As time goes on you feel uncertain about what you have already done and need to rethink. And, of course, at any one time-point the future, and thus the whole picture, is unknown.

How, from the middle of this mess, can you keep control of your efforts and retain some kind of balance?

Try these three stabilizers:

1.   Recognize that this situation is *normal*. Research is never linear so don't expect it to be so.
2.   Keep a diary and use it to reflect on how your time and effort are being spent.
3.   Talk regularly and frequently to your supervisor. Exploit your supervisor's experience and get his or her view on the time you are spending.

Finally, you might prefer to view your project as progressing by gentle curves:

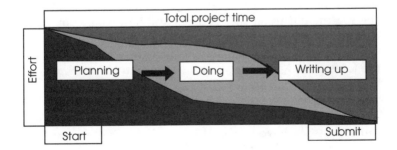

Bottom line

Research is neither simple nor linear. A productive project will give few opportunities for single-mindedness but will give many for unexpected good fortune. *Expect* the parts to overlap and form an untidy sequence but keep the *total* effort in balance.

SPREADING THE LOAD

In Chapter 3, we considered the problems associated with balancing project work against the other demands of your course. Now that you are working on the project itself, time management becomes a question of organizing your research effort so that the components of the study come together at the right time and in the correct proportions. What you may not be able to see too clearly from this distance is how the key elements (designing, reading, measuring, recording, writing, etc.) of the work will distribute themselves over the full period of the project. And, without knowing the final sum, it's difficult to estimate in advance how much time each component should occupy.

Boxes 5.2 (page 52) and 5.3 (page 53) show a simple, two-stage approach to solving this problem. It begins by dividing the work under three broad headings (planning, doing, writing) and allocating equal amounts of the available time to each. Table 5.2 shows what each heading is intended to cover. You may feel that equal allocation of time in this way is a risky oversimplification. Experience shows, however, that it is reasonably realistic for most projects and most students. You have no other way of predicting how long each part of your own project will take. In the absence of hindsight on your personal situation, it is therefore a sensible way to proceed.

The situation described in Box 5.3 is probably, but not inevitably, how things will turn out. Like all plans, this one needs flexibility in the execution. The final proportions will depend on factors which you can't anticipate at the outset such as:

❐   your aptitude for planning, doing and writing;
❐   the size and accessibility of the existing literature base;
❐   the routine nature of the methods and how easily you can adapt them;
❐   the complexity of the analyses you have to perform;
❐   the foresight which your planning turns out to have had.

Nevertheless, splitting your time into three roughly equal parts is what you should be aiming for so be as strict with yourself as possible: if you unexpectedly have to spend longer than you wanted to on one part, make up for it later on.

Table 5.2 Components of project time	
Thirds of total project time	*Activity*
1. Planning	Thinking about the idea
	Discussions with supervisor
	Discussion with other staff
	Reading background literature
	Getting additional information
	Developing a working hypothesis
	Designing experiments
	Making predictions
2. Doing	Sifting, analysing and synthesizing existing information and data
	Reading detailed literature
	Learning methods and procedures
	Developing new methods and procedures
	Applying methods and getting results
	Analysing data
	Creating the product
	Writing interim reports
	Interpreting results and drawing conclusions
3. Writing up	Writing, reviewing and re-writing
	Preparing data and diagrams
	Listing references
	Formatting and error checking
	Copying and binding

RISK

Research is a risky business: you have no way of knowing at the outset what the result will be. Professional researchers accept that this risk goes with the territory. It makes their lives both exciting and precarious, but they made their own career choices and need no sympathy.

In your case, the responsibilities for risk-taking are not quite so clear. As discussed earlier, exposing you to uncertainty in the midst of more solid academic pursuits is one of the reasons for getting you to do some research in the first place. It would therefore be downright misleading and wrong to give you a project whose outcome was certain. On the other hand, the project should not be so ill-defined that the chance of getting a substantial result is remote.

However much the project idea came from you, the final responsibility for the project and its risks (of time, effort and consumables) must rest with your supervisor. This is not a problem, provided you discuss things at each stage. But, of course, it does not absolve you from the responsibility of doing your utmost to complete the work. A supervisor could be blamed for misleading you into thinking that a sample size of five will do when 100 would be more reasonable, but you have only yourself to blame if you only complete one 20th of a previously agreed amount of work.

REDUCING RISK: THE RESEARCH PLAN

The need to create a good working relationship with your supervisor has been mentioned before and cannot be overstressed. Part of the process of that relationship involves the construction and application of a **research plan**. This document (which need not be over-formal) records your agreed approach and methodology but also provides a yardstick against which to measure progress. To function effectively, the work plan must be a working document. It is not to be tucked away in a drawer and forgotten, neither should it be seen as threatening. Look at it regularly and use it as the basis for discussions with your supervisor. Make an honest and objective comparison between what is happening in the work and the progress which you both anticipated: progress is as likely to have been underestimated as overestimated. Adjust your plan if that seems appropriate, provided that you do not lose sight of the main purpose.

Setting and reviewing a **research plan** is one way to guard against the risk of overcommitment. It is difficult (impossible) to know at the outset how much work you will be able to complete. One of the assumptions of this book is that you are doing your project alongside other work, probably for a degree, and the value of effective time management skills has been discussed earlier. So, in your research plan you need to be realistic about your workload related to the project **together with** your overall workload. You will undoubtedly surprise yourself at your productivity as the project progresses but if things do start to get out of control don't be afraid of reviewing your overall circumstances as well as the details of your research work.

DISTINGUISHING BETWEEN FAILURE AND LACK OF SUCCESS

You will be relieved to learn that very few student projects fail. That is to say, most projects are reasonably well planned, enthusiastically executed and reach their natural and anticipated end. This is different from saying that most projects are completely successful. 'Complete success' means 'Proceed without a hitch from the initial hypothesis to a predicted and secure conclusion of great moment'. Few projects go as well as this: if they did, there would be no challenge and consequently little point in using them as a teaching or learning method.

A failed project would be one in which there is nothing (really, nothing) valuable to show for the time spent – one in which the participants felt they had wasted resources and worked without purpose. The difference can be seen in Table 5.3.

Table 5.3   Distinguishing between failure and lack of success

	The outcome	Your attitude	How you present it to others
Lack of success	❑ Unexpected results ❑ Unworkable product ❑ Less information than anticipated ❑ Unable properly to test the hypothesis	❑ Seeking explanations and gaining understanding ❑ Reappraisal for future improvement ❑ Generation of a new hypothesis	❑ As an undesirable or unexpected, but nevertheless *defensible* and *explicable*, or *potentially explicable*, outcome
Failure	❑ No results ❑ No product ❑ No information ❑ No test of the hypothesis	❑ Seeking a list of excuses ❑ Abandoning interest	❑ As a series of apologies

However well your project goes, there will be some elements of it that you (from your privileged position of insider) find less satisfying than others. You will be aware of holes and deficiencies in the work which even your supervisor would find difficult to spot. Despite your personal integrity, you will most probably want to keep quiet about these and put the best possible spin on the outcome. This does not mean that the project failed. It means that you went through a legitimate intellectual process, during the course of which new information, insight and understanding were obtained.

Developing a feel for the difference between failure and lack of success is crucial to the maintenance of your own motivation. You have no time to do the work again, so your aim in planning the project with your supervisor must be to ensure a worthwhile outcome. Whatever you do, don't be left with the feeling that the project failed because of bad planning, laziness or poor workmanship.

PRE-EMPTING DISASTER

It is quite possible that at some time during the course of your project you will start to feel that things are falling apart or that you are losing control. You may start to feel:

❑   that you are unavoidably spending disproportionate amounts of time on parts of the study;
❑   that you can't get your methods to work;
❑   that matters outside your project are hindering progress;
❑   that the results are failing to come;
❑   that your results don't show anything;
❑   that you are losing touch with what you should be doing.

Specific advice on dealing with these feelings is given in the section 'Maintaining sanity' in Chapter 7 on page 108 (although the general recommendation in all such cases of uncertainty is: speak immediately to your supervisor). What you can do during the planning stage of your project is think ahead a little and take steps to make these feelings less likely.

It is not uncommon, for example, for students to underestimate the time taken for writing up and to spend too long on the practical work. It is far better to do some effective planning, get a smaller amount of more focused work completed and present what you have done in a proper manner, than to do a rushed job. Most supervisors will fully appreciate the limited amount of time you have to play with. One of their roles is to look over your shoulder and monitor progress objectively. This includes fitting project work into your busy academic schedule, as discussed earlier. They will, on the one hand, recognize when routine items are taking longer than anticipated to complete and, on the other, curtail both your enthusiasm and their own when you start getting too carried away with the excitement of it all.

■ DESIGN AND DETAILED PLANNING

Project design has four complementary elements:

1. Establishing what needs to be done;
2   Working out how to do it;
3. Determining how much you can get done;
4. Predicting and interpreting the outcome.

These elements are all matters for discussion with your supervisor. He or she should understand the field well enough to know whether you are sufficiently informed before you start, and will also have some idea about what you should be capable of and what resources will allow.

1 and 2. Working out what needs to be done and how to do it
These elements are largely objective and a matter of self-education. They require you to immerse yourself in the subject and become an active participant. You need to be informed as thoroughly as possible about the precise nature of the question being asked, about the methods you need to answer it and about how to make best use of the answer you obtain. Information comes from:

❏   Reading the literature;
❏   Talking to others;
❏   Dialogue with your supervisor;
❏   Thinking hard.

3. Working out how much you can do
This element is more subjective and relates to your personal circumstances. It is no good being too ambitious – that just leads to disappointment and frustration. On the other hand, you need to get through a worthwhile amount of work if you are to achieve anything at all. You should expect to stretch yourself, so lean towards over- rather than underestimation of what you are capable of, but be realistic and take the advice of your supervisor. You should be able to:

❏   work out a reasonable design framework which is robust enough to carry you through;
❏   fill the spaces in the framework with detailed plans for each task or component of the study.

The tasks and components of your project are subject-specific and little general advice can be given. Your supervisor is your best advisor in these matters. It is wise, however, to work out the level of certainty which is attached to each one. Try completing a 'QRS' grid (Box 5.4) as a means of clearing the mind and sorting your ideas out.

Box 5.4   The QRS grid for project planning

This grid will help you analyse and organize your thoughts and ideas. It will help you work out what is possible now and what you need to do to make other things possible in the future. It is similar to the so-called 'SWOT' analysis in which you reflect on your correct Strengths and Weaknesses, and on current Opportunities for and Threats to progress. The main difference is that QRS concentrates on tasks rather than personal feelings. It also makes you look forward and encourages you to plan for what is required.

❑   List the things you have to do in the first column of the grid. Give them a rough order of precedence in column 2. If there is an expected completion date or a deadline you need to work to, add this in column 2 as well.

❑   Now, in column 3, use one of the following categories to describe how successful you think the task would be if you did it *today, now, in your present state of mind and knowledge*:
   Q Quite likely to succeed
   R Risky, but worth attempting
   S Stupid, even to try (at this stage)

❑   For each item labelled 'R' or 'S', jot down some notes in explanation. These could refer to:
   – further information you need to find
   – help you need to ask for
   – resources that are not yet available
   – things that need to happen first

❑   Revisit the chart from time to time as a means of reflecting on progress.

Component or task	Order of precedence	Q R S	Notes

4. Predicting and interpreting the outcome

An essential part of any planning process is predicting the outcome. What you need is some kind of expected result against which to measure your achievement. Traditionally, scientific experiments build this into the statistical analysis, but the principle applies equally well to all kinds of research activity. Look ahead and, knowing the question you started out with, work out what kinds of possible answer you might get. Box 5.5 shows some of the reasons why predictions are valuable.

Box 5.5   Seven reasons for predicting the outcome of your project before you start

❏   To make you ask yourself whether the question is a sensible one:
-   'Can I formulate the question properly, succinctly and coherently?'
-   'Will the answer tell me something new?'

❏   To make you work out whether the hypothesis you have constructed is properly testable:
-   'Will the data I collect allow me to reject the hypothesis, if that is what is called for?'
-   'Have I set up the right control?'

❏   To help you to work out whether you have available all the resources and techniques you will need:
-   'Am I able to carry out the work properly?'
-   'Will I be totally self-reliant or dependent on someone else's contribution?'

❏   To enable you to decide, particularly in scientific experiments, whether you have built enough replication into the design:
-   'Will I be able to carry out and complete the appropriate experimental analysis?'
-   'Will I be able to draw conclusions from the outcome?'

❏   To allow you to distinguish between 'failure' and 'lack of success' (see p. 57):
-   'How will I recognize and distinguish useful/conclusive results?'
-   'What will my emotional response be to each of the possible outcomes?'

❏   To be sure that you have the answer you want:
-   'What is the answer to my question likely to look like?'
-   'How will I know when I have finished?'

❏   To know when to be genuinely surprised and excited:
-   'Should I trust, accept or ignore this result?'
-   'Is this the moment to shout "Eureka!" or will I just make a fool of myself?'

Predictions are best made in the form of **thought experiments** such as these:

☐   Make a sketch of what you think the finished product might look like; make several sketches if the product might take one of several different forms;

or

☐   Draw a set of graphs to show all the possible shapes of response to the treatment you are giving (don't forget to include the curve illustrating 'no response');

or   .

☐   Draw up a chart of the experimental design and indicate where the most likely significant effects will be;

or

☐   Talk to a statistician about the tests you are going to apply and find out if your design will allow you to do them.

And then

☐   Think about how you will **interpret** and **react to** each of the possible outcomes you have predicted.

It is very important that these activities are done before you start. They should not cause anxiety: 'How do I know if my idea is going to work?', 'What if it takes longer than expected?', 'What if it all falls apart?'

These unpalatable options should be among the possibilities you deal with before you start. Put them on your list of potential outcomes. If you do this, you will be able to prepare for them and deal with them. You will also make them less likely to happen.

The need for prediction may be hard to appreciate in some circumstances. You may feel, for example:

☐   that lack of experience prevents you from anticipating the outcome;

☐   that you want to get on with the work and see what the results show before imagining them;

☐   that you want to wait to see the outcome before thinking about the interpretation;

☐   that the analytical tests you apply will be determined by the shape of the data and cannot be chosen in advance;

☐   that making predictions will prevent you from observing the unexpected.

These are *bad* approaches. They are almost guaranteed to induce failure and should be avoided at all costs. If you find possible outcomes hard to imagine, read some more literature or talk further with your supervisor. Remember:

- If you go ahead with the work without knowing what to expect, you will miss important information and come to erroneous conclusions.
- The best way to upset a statistician is to ask for advice on experimental design **after** getting the data rather than **before**.
- You can only be prepared for and observe the unexpected if the expected has already been accounted for.

DETAILED RESEARCH DESIGN

The specific methods you use to design and carry out your research will be determined by your subject area. The quality of the information you obtain will depend directly on the quality of the research methods you use. Apparently simple matters, such as sample size or the availability of evidential cross-references (sometimes called 'triangulation'), can make all the difference between reliable and unreliable conclusions. These matters need to be built into your research at the design stage.

As well as discussing these matters with your supervisor, you may wish to consult some of the books in the Bibliography. If your work involves questionnaires or interviews look particularly at Allison *et al.* (1996), Bell (1993) or Blaxter *et al.* (1996). Advice on experimental design in the sciences, on statistics and on other matters related to numerical data is provided by Lumley and Benjamin (1994), Martin and Bateson (1993), and Pechenik and Lamb (1994). This Bibliography is by no means exhaustive and your library will doubtless have a well-stocked section relevant to your requirements.

ANALYSIS OF NUMERICAL DATA

Research involving numbers is special. If you can measure something, as distinct from just describing it, you have the potential to produce information of much higher quality. The late astronomer and philosopher Carl Sagan (1997) put this eloquently:

> If you know a thing only qualitatively, you know it no more
> than vaguely. If you know it quantitatively – grasping some
> numerical measure that distinguishes it from an infinite
> number of other possibilities – you are beginning to know it
> deeply. Being afraid of quantitation is tantamount to disen-
> franchising yourself.

Not all academic disciplines lend themselves to quantitation but if
yours does you should make the most of the opportunity. Even if you
struggled with maths at school and have deliberately avoided engaging
with it ever since, don't reject numbers now just because of unfamiliarity. You will be surprised how much more interesting and accessible
numbers become once you have your own data and measurements to
work on.

If you are doing a project which unavoidably involves numerical
data, statistics will already play a big part in your life. Part of your formal course will probably have been devoted to statistics, data analysis
and experimental design. Note that Sagan refers to '. . . grasping some
numerical measure that distinguishes it from an infinite number of
other possibilities'. In other words, your data needs to be justified
statistically so that you and others know how reliable it is.

Academic courses in these subjects are universally recognized for
their mind-numbing tedium and soporific effects. But they are hard
to avoid. The people who designed your course put those modules in
for the best of motives but probably got an expert statistician to
teach them. While that was a sensible thing to do from the point of view
of academic rigour, it was (unless you were very fortunate in your
choice of lectures!) possibly not the best way of endearing you to the
subject.

The great thing, however, is that statistical analysis can become
your greatest friend and staunchest ally once you have occasion to
apply them to **your own data**. It can even be **fun to do**. Often, the
best people to teach practical statistics are not statisticians but working scientists, engineers, epidemiologists and social scientists. In other
words, those who use statistical techniques as an everyday tool. These
people will have learned their ANOVAs, Mann-Whitney tests and
orthogonal contrasts as you will learn them: not from dry statistical
textbooks but by doing the work, producing the data and using the
analysis to get answers to important, real questions.

Statistical tests are complex things, even when fully automated.
They often have obscure historical names which say little if anything
about function. The Kolmogorov-Smirnoff test, for example, may sound
like a quality control assay in a vodka factory but turns out to be an
indispensable way of determining whether a set of observations is nor-

mally distributed. Similarly, the terminology used to describe variables and parameters may be set in unfamiliar statistician-speak. Often the outcome of the test itself can be cryptic.

But don't fret. Assuming that you have sat through lectures on the basic principles, you should be able to learn the mechanics of the tests you need as you need them. But that is not the same thing as leaving it until it is too late to find out what you need. The advice is worth repeating: 'Get statistical advice at the design stage, before you start generating **any** data.'

This is not a book on statistics or experimental design and does not presume to offer advice on either. But there is just one further thing to add. Statistical tests, whatever their complexity or apparent obscurity, demand a **predicted outcome**. They demand that you have:

- ❑ a 'null hypothesis';
- ❑ a sufficient number of examples of the phenomenon to test your hypothesis, and;
- ❑ some means of determining what **chance** looks like.

These matters can, and must, be dealt with *before* you start work. If you are doing a numerical project of any kind, improving your knowledge of statistics will automatically improve the design and outcome of your study.

Make your statistical advisor (whether professional statistician or practical user of statistical methods) your best friend and listen to what he or she has to say. Once you have your own questions to ask, the advice of the statistician suddenly becomes comprehensible, even interesting. Yes, even fun.

■ INFORMATION: ACCESS AND ETHICS

To do research, you need access to information. Some of the information you need will have been collected by others and your job will be to look at it with fresh eyes. Other information you will collect yourself; this will be entirely new material or material which has never been collected before in the way that you will do it. The fact that information exists or is obtainable does not, however, mean that you necessarily have an automatic right to obtain it or make use of it. Gaining access to information always incurs obligations. In designing your project, you need to be aware of the rights and responsibilities associated with each set of information you might need. You need to plan your work around information which can be collected legitimately and ethically.

For the present purpose, the information you might need can be divided into several categories under two headings. See Table 5.4.

Table 5.4 Categories of information	
Existing information *(Already collected by someone else)*	*New information* *(Newly collected by you)*
1. Published or in the public domain 2. Unpublished	3. Obtained from or with the help of other people 4. Obtained by experiment or observation, not involving other people or animals 5. Obtained by experiment with, or observation of, animals

Each of these categories carries a different level of responsibility as far as access and ethics are concerned.

1. Published information

Information which is published, for example in a book or journal, raises few issues concerning rights of access. Our society is based around the principles of liberal access to information (even if we do not yet have a specific Freedom of Information Act). The free transfer of information is one of the fundamental freedoms on which successful scholarship depends and academic life exploits this advantage to the full. This does not mean that all information is easy to get hold of but it does mean than no one can legitimately prevent you from trying to acquire it. Your access to information in the public domain is limited only by practical considerations such as the time and enthusiasm you have available, any costs which need to be met and the facilities offered by your library. (*Note:* A possible exception to this would be pornographic, libellous, blasphemous or otherwise offensive material which, though published or freely accessible in this country or abroad, is covered by national or local laws restricting its use. Information on the Internet may sometimes fall into the latter category where, for example, your university code of practice forbids the downloading of certain types of material.)

Although published information is freely available for academic use your use of it carries certain responsibilities. As a professional researcher, you will want to use your information wisely. This means presenting it fairly, and with due acknowledgement, and not using it out of context (see also the section 'Plagiarism and Fabrication' in Chapter 9 on page 145). You also have a moral responsibility not to use it deliberately to offend individuals or groups. While facts may be neutral, facts do not really exist: what you have is information. Information is subjective and value-laden. Others may not share your interpretation of it, so treat it with care.

2. Unpublished information
This is the property of the person who collected it and you need their permission in order to use it. How you set about getting permission depends on the nature of the information but, as a general rule, a written statement acknowledging your right of access is the only safe way of protecting yourself against later charges of plagiarism, fraud or breach of copyright. You need to be quite clear about what 'access' means, (citing?, copying?, summarizing?, publishing?, acknowledgement in publication?) and also that the person giving you the permission to access it has the authority to do so. For example, if you need to search a physical archive of some kind you need to make sure that you:

❐   have permission to enter;
❐   know how far you may search;
❐   when and for how long;
❐   know what you may and may not remove;
❐   obtain additional, express permission to copy, publish or cite the material.

Although this all sounds daunting and legalistic, don't be put off. It is basically common sense. Provided you are honest and open about what you want to do, most guardians of information will be flattered by your interest and will try their best to be helpful. Be tenacious and persistent in your enquiries but at the same time be polite, be respectful and know when to stop.

Above all, talk to your supervisor before you start and take the advice which is offered. Your supervisor has overall responsibility for what you are doing so make sure that he or she is kept fully informed about and sanctions your actions. Mention your supervisor in letters you write to outside agencies and provide him or her with copies to file. It is unfair to expect your supervisor to vouch for your legitimacy if you have not discussed your intentions beforehand.

ETHICAL ISSUES

INVOLVING OTHERS

Much research work involves collecting new information from or with the help of other people. Here are some examples of what you might want to do:

- ❐ survey opinions or attitudes (sociology, politics);
- ❐ measure personal attributes (psychology, physiology, behavioural science);
- ❐ gauge reactions (marketing, product analysis);
- ❐ ascertain the requirements of a brief (design, engineering, artistic commission).

Start by asking yourself the question: 'Is anyone else affected by what I am about to do?'. If the answer, however hesitantly, is 'Yes' then you should carry out an **ethical analysis** of what you have in mind. Box 5.6 suggests the further questions you might need to ask.

If your research is to be carried out alone and doesn't involve anyone else, then your ethical responsibilities are substantially reduced. This might be the case for much laboratory experimentation, for some environmental fieldwork or for projects which depend entirely on published information. Nevertheless, you still need an awareness of the use to which your information might be put and you owe it to yourself and to your supervisor to be as professional as possible in what you do and not to waste resources. You might well consider these to be matters of ethics, or at least of moral and social responsibility.

Box 5.6   Ask ELSI (ethical, legal, social issues)

Questions to ask about the ethical, legal and social issues related to your work.

Informed consent
- ❐ How can I be sure that my subjects are willing to be involved?
- ❐ Am I exerting any subtle or unfair pressure on my subjects to take part (for example, use of family members, colleagues; reciprocal agreements)?
- ❐ Do they know what to expect by taking part in the study?
- ❐ Do they have a clear statement of their rights and obligations?
- ❐ How much background information do I need to give them (and will this affect the quality of the data I obtain)?
- ❐ Are there any personal risks that they need to be made aware of?

Box 5.6   Continued

☐   Do they have the opportunity to withdraw from the study at any time without giving a reason?

Confidentiality

☐   Are my subjects happy for information about them to be made pulic?
☐   Will they be telling me things which would normally be kept private?
☐   Have my subjects the right to ask me not to use, and to destroy, particular pieces of information if they so wish?
☐   Will my subjects have a chance to confirm that the information I have recorded about them is factually correct?

Anonymity

☐   Have I taken care to ensure that my sources of data are not identifiable as individuals to anyone outside the study team?
☐   Can any piece of circumstantial information uniquey identify one individual?
☐   Am I sure that the origin of individual items of data will not be externally traceable?
☐   Will the fact that subjects have been recruited to the study serve to identify them as belonging to a particular (social, medical, ethnic) group?

Legality

☐   Does the study raise any legal questions?
☐   What will my attitude be to information which appears to result from or reflect criminal activity?
☐   Could the data I obtain expose any of the subjects to legal risk?
☐   Have I obtained approval for my study from my local ethical committee?
☐   Is my supervisor fully aware of what I intend to do and prepared to take responsibility?
☐   Who will own the information or final product that is produced?

Professionalism

☐   Does the study need to be done: am I sure that the data I want does not exist already?
☐   Have I got the right number of subjects: will I have sufficient data to justify my conclusions or, alternatively, will I be involving more subjects than I require? (Have I obtained adequate statistical advice?)
☐   Is the study properly designed and have I got the analytical techniques I need?
☐   Am I prepared to treat my subjects with courtesy and respect, even if I find their views or habits personally objectionable?
☐   Have I arranged appropriate support if things go wrong?
☐   Have I given the commissioning organization a realistic timetable for completion?

USING ANIMALS

In the biological and medical sciences, the issue of **animal experimentation** raises special ethical and legal questions. Here you certainly *do not* have an automatic right to all information in the sense that what you may or may not do is governed by the law, by social norms and by personal attitudes. It is of paramount importance that your experiments are acceptable within the terms of the Animals (Scientific Procedures) Act 1986. Your supervisor will explain what is necessary and will make sure that you have appropriate training, guidance and, if necessary, licensing. In fact it is extremely unlikely that, as an undergraduate, you would be allowed to carry out procedures covered by the Act.

It is more likely that you will be required to work in association with a qualified, licensed person. If this is the case, you should inform yourself about the procedure as fully as possible and exercise the same levels of care and professionalism as if you were the responsible individual. This includes planning your work thoroughly and using the minimum number of animals compatible with gathering useful data, as well as avoiding the infliction of undue pain or suffering. Consider this as professional training: knowing the correct way to handle and treat your animals is a key component of experimental methodology and cannot be isolated from the process of obtaining experimental data.

Where your experimental animals are not specifically covered by the Act (invertebrates, for example), you will still want to cause as little pain or suffering as possible. Your actions are still subject to the strictures of your own conscience, to acceptance by the local ethical committee and to social and institutional convention. Remember, however, that you might be called upon at any time to describe what you are doing to other people. They may not share either your background knowledge, enthusiasm or moral assumptions. Remember also that you will eventually be called upon to justify your research to your examiners. You will be judged as much on your approach and planning as on the results you have obtained.

■ THE ETHICAL MATRIX

The gathering of information in categories 3 and 5 of Table 5.4 requires you to exercise significant ethical judgement. This can be tough to do without guidance, however thoughtful and conscientious you try to be. The Ethical Matrix, originally developed at the

University of Nottingham in the context of animal and food biotechnology (Mepham, 1996), can be helpful in deciding where your responsibilities lie.

To create a matrix, draw a grid with column headings as follows: interest groups; beneficence (provision of benefits); non-maleficence (avoidance of harm); autonomy; justice (a fair distribution of benefits, risks and costs). Fill in the interests groups column using as wide an interpretation as possible. Next, work across the matrix filling in the gaps with short statements appropriate to each potential ethical interaction. Finally, use the information in the matrix to balance the ethical costs and benefits of the proposed work. Box 5.7 gives a couple of examples of how the matrix might develop.

The matrix forces a consideration of how each of the parties with an interest in the work (Y-axis) is affected by each of several ethical principles (X-axis) according to 'common sense' morality and democratic agreement. In establishing these relationships, the matrix tries to balance the potential gains to be derived from a particular activity or

Box 5.7 The Ethical Matrix

Example 1: The physiology of exercise (human subjects)

Interest groups	Beneficence	Non-maleficence	Autonomy	Justice
Subjects on a rowing machine	Opportunity to gain knowledge of personal fitness Nominal payment	Safe equipment Controlled conditions Medical supervision Emergency back-up	Voluntary participation Right to withdraw at any time	Monitored stress level and adequate recovery time Expenses reimbursed Anonymous presentation of data
Medical supervisors	Opportunity for paid professional work	Fully briefed Responsibilities clearly stated Emergency back-up	Right to intervene medically at own discretion	Timetables arranged to suit Workload shared equitably
Project student (you!)	Acquisition of data to test hypothesis Advancement of knowledge and skills	Ethical committee approval Adequate supervision Advice on design from statistician	Control of project design and execution	Adequate resources provided by department

Example 2: Mathematical education in primary schools (class observation)

Interest groups	Beneficence	Non-maleficence	Autonomy	Justice
School pupils	Additional personal attention	Provision of written information to parents Avoidance of distraction and interruption to learning	Right of parents to withdraw child from study	Equitable distribution of attention
Teacher of class under observation	Additional personnel in school and help with class Recognition of professional work	Avoidance of interruption to teaching	Freedom to ask student to stop work or leave at any time	Opportunity to view outcome before publication Right to request anonymity
School teaches in general	Information on best/ comparative practice	Public recognition of professional activity	Opportunity for professional body to examine and comment on aims, objectives and methods	Designing study to ensure fairness and equality of representation
University department	Data towards completion of a multi-centre study	Prior planning of project to ensure value of data Thorough training of project student	Right to withdraw student from study if he or she is not appropriate	
Project student	Acquisition of data to test hypothesis Advancement of knowledge and skills	Adequate supervision Advice on design from statistician	Day-to-day management of study within class Opportunity for regular feedback and consultation from supervisor	Reimbursement of travel expenses Recognition of time spent away from university

endeavour against the personal and extra-personal risks and suffering which might be involved. In the case of studies involving animals, besides using the ethical matrix, consider applying the 3Rs of Reduction, Refinement and Replacement to the design of your experiments.

Construct an ethical matrix for your project if you think it would be helpful. It would certainly be a good item to include in any feasibility study you are asked to produce. In using it, remember that not all the points of intersection in the matrix will carry equal weight: some may be trivial while others assume an overriding significance. There may be occasions when obligations appear to conflict. Other situations may have no ethical implications. In other words, the matrix is 'ethically neutral' and its outcome remains open to your subjective evaluation and your social and institutional circumstances. The matrix will not answer your ethical questions for you but it may help you to analyse them more thoroughly.

DOING IT

CHAPTER

6

READING THE LITERATURE

WHY SO MUCH LITERATURE?

To do useful research you need to know what other people have already done. Your subject has an established body of knowledge on which current views, hypotheses and dogma are based. There are five main reasons for needing to read, study, understand and (in some cases) remember this literature:

- ☐ so that you know where the gaps in current knowledge are;
- ☐ so that you don't re-invent any existing wheels;
- ☐ so that what you do is either a logical extension or a properly informed criticism of what has been done before;
- ☐ so that you avoid mistakes and blind alleys which others have already discovered;
- ☐ so that you can acknowledge and make proper reference to previous work.

These reasons apply to **anyone** doing **any** research under **any** circumstances.

There are other reasons which apply specifically to you as a student trying to get a good degree:

- ☐ you will want to be able to answer questions confidently and knowledgeably when presenting your work;
- ☐ your supervisor will expect to hold informed conversations with you about what may well be his or her pet topic;
- ☐ it will help to improve your writing style;
- ☐ the ability to 'drop' names and dates will give you confidence and encourage feelings of ownership of the subject;

❑   some part of your degree assessment, probably involving external as well as internal examiners, will relate to your knowledge of the literature.

The size of the literature base, even for topics which seem relatively obscure or esoteric, can be daunting. And of course it is increasing all the time as new papers, books and articles are published. You are expected to bone up on the background of an unfamiliar subject but at the same time read and understand the mountains of new stuff which keep appearing – an almost impossible task.

If it is any comfort, it is very unlikely that your supervisor has more than a passing familiarity with most of it. He or she will know the main material in great detail (and may even impress you by being able to quote you the authors' initials and journal page numbers!) and be acquainted with a substantially larger amount of it in rather less detail. But much of what has been read over the years will have been ignored, forgotten or superseded. That is to be expected. Being an 'expert' includes the frequent application of a selective memory and being 'selectively negligent' is a key research skill which you too will acquire. And of course, your supervisor has other sources of information about what is going on (attending conferences, personal correspondence with others in the field, etc.).

Experienced researchers are highly skilled in selecting what to read, what to read more than once and what to remember. Research papers are seldom read from cover to cover – a glance at a title or a skim through an abstract may be all that is required to allow placement of the next piece in the jigsaw. Anyone already involved in a subject and doing their own research is in a good position to be critical and selective. You are not yet in that position but you are moving rapidly towards it. The question is: 'How do I get from here to there without losing too many precious marbles?'

 FINDING THE LITERATURE

Tracking down the right literature to read and assimilate usually has two stages. **Stage 1** is a process of reconnoitre. It sometimes gets to feel like a waste of time but it is a necessary pre-requisite to **Stage 2** which is the more clearly productive stage. You will chase several shoals of red herring and many flocks of wild geese before the first part of the hunt is over, but don't dismay. Very often, knowing what you are not looking for is as valuable as finding the correct material straight away.

Before getting hold of any literature you need to know where to look for it:

❑ Your institution library is your natural point of departure (Box 6.1) so make sure your registration details are up to date and that your access card is where you think it is. Avail yourself of training in how to use the library NOW, if you have not already done so. Talk to library staff. Locate the in-house guides on everything from book classification systems and CD-ROMs to word-processing and prose style.

❑ Talk to your supervisor about any specialist archives of literature outside the institution to which you might need access.

❑ Your department may have an eclectic collection of journals, catalogues, learned society publications and other specialist literature. Ask to see it and find out about borrowing facilities.

❑ Academic members of the department will have their own personal collections of key papers and articles. If your subject is closely related to one of their interests, and you can establish an appropriately friendly relationship, they may be able to save you some foot-slogging and inter-library loan requests.

FINDING THE LITERATURE

Stage 1 – Where to start

Try the following techniques to get a foothold in the literature of a new subject. Your aim at this stage should be to inform yourself about the scope of the subject rather than to locate the fine detail. Make some rough notes about what you find and draw lines to link up the various ideas you think you might use.

❑ Ask your **supervisor** to point you to some key texts. This seems obvious, and will probably happen anyway, but there is no harm in asking. Your supervisor may not be sure about where the gaps in your general knowledge are and may need some prompting to give you the right key references. Don't be afraid of asking stupid questions – no one is keeping a record!

❑ Look in graduate/postgraduate level **textbooks**. These often have short bibliographies at the end of each chapter listing key references. Make sure, however, that the books are relatively recent: the average textbook can takes two years or more to pass from author to library shelf. Some of the textbook-like volumes in the library may turn out to be collections of symposium papers or reviews and these can be especially useful in indicating the scope of the subject, even if you find their level of detail difficult to deal with.

Box 6.1	Where to look for the literature

Your institution library
Right of access comes courtesy of your student registration (this applies to all parts of the library, which might turn out to be larger than you think). Can be a gateway to other libraries, including the British Library Document Supply Centre, through the inter-library loan scheme. Will probably facilitate access to on-line databases held elsewhere.

Other libraries
Public libraries; national collections; museum libraries; private collections; learned society archives. Ask your library staff for advice on contact and access.

Library sections

❏ Open shelves: Reference works, monographs, conference summaries, student texts, popular texts, recreational fiction (if you are lucky). Can be borrowed. Catalogued using one of two alphanumeric class systems: Library of Congress or (rarely) Dewey Decimal; both systems are logical and straightforward to use; the library will provide training and/or guidance notes on its own system.

❏ Reference: Dictionaries, encyclopaedias, directories, maps, atlases, data compendia, catalogues, newspapers, magazines, supplements. Borrowing not usually permitted.

❏ Periodicals: Separate section of bound or box-filed journal holdings. Arranged alphabetically by title, then by year, volume and part. Catalogue lists the titles held and indicates the completeness of the collection. Borrowing limited or by special arrangement. Copies of the most recent issues are probably displayed in a separate area for browsing.

❏ Bibliography: Abstracting and citation journals and their indices; listings of current research literature, for example, current contents; periodical directories. Increasing tendency for this material to be based on CD-ROMs and on-line databases. An indispensable resource area for researchers needing to keep up to date.

❏ Dissertations: Copies of all doctoral and other postgraduate theses produced within the institution. Inter-library loan scheme can obtain copies of theses from other institutions worldwide.

Box 6.1   Continued

❏   Stack: Rare/precious volumes and manuscripts; out-of-date material; ancient periodical sets. Usually held in a basement, attic or separate building. Listed in main catalogue but access may be by special request to staff.

Library catalogues
Usually accessed through user-friendly computer terminals. Previously based on file cards, printed volumes and microfiche, and remnants of such systems may still be in use. Searchable by author, subject, title, keyword, classification numbers, etc., may offer direct links to on-line databases, the inter-library loan scheme and even your personal library details.

Librarians
Wonderful people: friendly, approachable, unexpectedly knowledgeable and full of surprises. Have the world of information (electronic as well as paper) at their fingertips. Often turn out to be subject specialists as well as information gurus. Invariably busy but delighted to be (politely) interrupted by requests for directions, advice and help.

❏   Once you have located a relevant section of the library, check along the **shelves** for related material. This kind of physical, serendipitous searching can be enormously rewarding (and is one reason why, whatever the influence of technology on the information world, paper-based libraries will never die!).

❏   Look at **review journals**, especially those that try to round up the subject area on an annual basis. Some ordinary journals also run occasional critical reviews and summaries of current topics, often as prefatory articles. As with library shelves, lateral browsing through these sources can throw up unexpected gems.

❏   Get hold of recent undergraduate or postgraduate **dissertations** from the department. These, especially the latter, will contain exhaustive surveys of the literature, parts of which may be just what you are looking for.

❏   Use **on-line research tools**, but use them sparingly and circumspectly at this stage. Until you have read around a little, you may have great difficulty in constructing an effective keyword search profile. It is easy to end up with either nothing or far too much, and to become disheartened in the process. When using on-line searches, a useful trick for locating general surveys of the literature in a particular area is to add '+review' or '+survey' (using syntax appropriate to your particular search engine) to your list of keywords. Set the search range to include Abstract as well as Title. This strategy sometimes throws up papers which are not in themselves review articles but which contain a brief summary of the latest research, perhaps as part of the introduction.

❑ Search the **Internet**. You may be lucky and find a web site or discussion group devoted directly to your topic. It would be rare for this to tell you anything of great research value but it may help to inform you about where the main developments in your field are taking place. More likely is that you will pick up references to personal research pages put up by students, academics, research groups or libraries in other universities or research centres around the world. Many academics put up their lecture notes on the web and produce interactive computer-aided learning (CAL) packages. These sources can give you references to methods, summaries of recent findings and researchers' names to look out for. They will also give you a useful feel for the topicality of your subject. You might find some surprising contextual uses of your otherwise narrowly defined research area.

❑ *Encyclopaedia Britannica.* A surprisingly useful starting point for many investigations, especially in an area you are not familiar with. Your library probably holds a more or less up-to-date edition. A CD-ROM version is available.

In this first stage of literature searching it is wise to concentrate exclusively on **secondary** rather than **primary** sources (Box 6.2). These are works which select, summarize, edit or in some other way **evaluate** the information on which your subject rests. In other words, rely at this stage on the guidance of others rather than trying to interpret the evidence for yourself. Once you have found your way through and around this (extensive) material you will be in a much better position to make informed assessments of the real primary data on which your research will depend.

Stage 2 – How to continue

Once you have opened your mind to the scope of the subject, you can start to assimilate information in a more focused manner. It is a good idea to make a **conscious** decision to move from Stage 1 to Stage 2. This enables you to throw out useless peripheral material which you might have been hanging on to, to adopt a more effective reading style and to make your note-taking more efficient and reliable. You can continue to use the same techniques as in Stage 1, although now with a much more focused scope and with greatly refined keyword lists.

Box 6.2   Types of literature source

Primary sources
- ❐ Original articles in research journals
- ❐ Research monographs
- ❐ Original books (factual, fictional)
- ❐ Conference reports and abstracts of conference presentations
- ❐ Survey reports
- ❐ Maps and charts
- ❐ Published photographs
- ❐ Original newspaper articles
- ❐ Government reports, statements and policy documents
- ❐ Law reports
- ❐ Patent descriptions
- ❐ Product descriptions
- ❐ Trade journals
- ❐ Monographs
- ❐ Dissertations (results and discussion sections)
- ❐ Original material from the Internet

Secondary sources
- ❐ Review articles in research journals
- ❐ Articles in review journals
- ❐ Review monographs
- ❐ Dissertations (literature survey section)
- ❐ Magazine articles
- ❐ Textbooks
- ❐ Product reviews
- ❐ Newspaper reviews

Reference sources
- ❐ Encyclopaedias
- ❐ Catalogues
- ❐ Handbooks and guides
- ❐ Directories
- ❐ Reference lists

Bibliographies
- ❐ Bibliographic journals
- ❐ Abstracting services (for example, BIDS, Medline, etc.)
- ❐ Indexing journals
- ❐ Current awareness services (paper, disk, on-line, etc.)
- ❐ Dissertations (bibliography section)

Move from reviews, surveys and summaries to the **primary litera-ture** (Box 6.2). This includes refereed research papers, reports, articles, etc. On-line searches and weekly or monthly abstracting journals/CD-ROMs will be your most useful source for locating these; ask the librarians for help if you are not sure how to proceed.

You will also have to start mining the **archives** of material, both published and unpublished, specific to your subject. These might include government documents, law reports, public enquiry reports, planning applications, letters, diaries, parish registers, accounts, ex-hibition catalogues, film and tape recordings, advertisements, indus-trial catalogues, pamphlets, to name but a few: no general advice can be given on how to tackle these, so consult your supervisor and other experts and be guided by their experience.

Try the following techniques for dealing with the primary research literature; they are not particularly original but they work:

❐   Whenever you read a paper in a journal, scan the **reference list** as a separate information-gathering exercise. Keep a list of all the references with relevant titles which you have not yet read. After every five or so papers that you consult, follow up all those refer-ences which have appeared in your list more than once. Repeat the process with those papers and so on. Avoid anything which looks too old or obscure for the remit of your study (don't get drawn into wasteful diversions from your main line of enquiry). This process will be laborious at first, but after a few iterations you will have narrowed the field considerably. After a surpris-ingly short time, the names of the leading or most prolific research groups in the field will be familiar to you and you will start to feel on top of the subject. You will start build up a mental stock of 'key' papers which are indispensable to a full understanding of the sub-ject and which anyone who has studied the field will be fully aware of. (You may even start to remember some publication details in just the way that your supervisor did to impress you earlier.)

❐   Select a few (two to four) journals which frequently publish useful papers on your subject. Scan the contents pages of these journals regularly, as they appear in the 'current issues' section of the library. Make sure that you never miss a new volume or part. Keep a checklist of part numbers in the back of a note book.

READING CRITICALLY: TRUST NO ONE

Now that you have started to gather first-hand information, your approach to reading needs to become much more **critical**. You must start to evaluate not only the **content** of the source you are reading but also its **reliability**.

The quality of published information is highly variable and nothing can be taken on trust. The fact that something is in print does not, of itself, guarantee reliability or veracity. Even the wisest, most senior of authorities have opinions which colour their judgement. And the fact that a particular view holds current sway does not mean that it is correct.

Your approach to ascertaining validity will depend on the nature of the source:

❐ Gauging the quality of articles in research journals is a relatively straightforward task: all such contributions will have been 'peer reviewed' which means that they have been subject to critical expert assessment before being accepted for publication. You can reasonably assume that this assessment was done in an informed and objective manner, although you will quickly discover that some journals publish material of a higher academic quality (content, originality, depth, topicality) than others. Furthermore, some journals have a wide international reputation while others have a much more limited standing: a glance at the list of editors will quickly inform you of the journal's constituency and likely academic position. A scan of authors' addresses will also be informative (but do **not** fall into the trap of dismissing or devaluing a paper on the basis of an unusual country of origin).

❐ Articles in newspapers, supplements, magazines and other popular media are not peer reviewed. The reliability of this information depends on the integrity of the writer and the diligence and selectivity of the editor. Be particularly wary of possible confusion between fact and opinion and remember that the emphasis and scope of an article may have been adjusted for editorial reasons. Editorial constraints on space can be lethally destructive as far as accuracy and precision are concerned, so read between the lines especially where crucial data are involved. Where possible, take full account of the author's position (editorial staff, occasional correspondent, freelance writer, commentator, etc.) and background (evidence of specialist qualifications, reputation, knowledge or experience) in coming to your conclusion. How objective are they likely to be? Might they have a hidden agenda? Is there an obvious political, social or gender bias? The most prolific writers are not necessarily the most reliable.

☐   Be especially careful of sources which go against the consensus – not because they are inevitably wrong but because the burden of proof needs to be that much greater if a current paradigm is to be successfully challenged. Consider the circumstances under which the material was assembled and ask searching questions: Why were these observations made or particular facts recorded? Did the authors have access to recent evidence? Did they use a representative sample? Was their investigative approach appropriate? Did they use the right controls? Was the information collected for one purpose but used for another? Has the information been used to test an hypothesis or to reinforce a prejudice? Was the work done for academic reasons or was it commercially sponsored? To what extent have the facts been summarized?

☐   **Review articles** (or comprehensive summaries of the literature within the body of another source) can be a useful guide to the reliability of existing literature. Any review worthy of the name should be a balanced summary of the various opinions available, not a catalogue of information. It should also come to some conclusion whose logic you can follow. You can then track the subsequent work of the authors whose publications have been cited and begin to judge for yourself how their work fits into the overall scheme of things. How well did a particular view or piece of information survive? Remember also that reviews are often at least 18 months out of date at the time they are published. And of course, reviewers themselves must be subject to your scrutiny. The 'totally objective opinion' is an oxymoron – there is no such thing.

LITERATURE: HAVE I COVERED IT ALL?

THE KNOWLEDGE MAP

☐   How long does my literature survey need to be?
☐   How many references do I need?
☐   How much is expected?
☐   When should I stop searching?

There are no simple answers to these frequently-asked questions. They depend on circumstantial factors such as the nature of your course and the expected length and depth of the project but also on subject-related factors. As in other discipline-specific matters, there is a mass of help and advice at hand in the form of your supervisor – you should consult him or her at every opportunity and pay heed to the advice provided. Previous examples of student projects will also show you what is possible and what is expected.

You may be able to concentrate your reading within an extensive and well-signposted body of knowledge. Alternatively, you may find yourself working with very limited information and only peripheral material to consult. Another common experience is to find yourself having to draw material from several abundant but previously disparate sources. In some subjects, the procedural details become paramount and your literature work involves delving into and comparing different methodological approaches. In other words, the size and diversity of your literature base is one of the defining characteristics of your subject. There is no finite amount (Box 6.3).

One thing to be very sure about is that covering the literature is not a competition – your examiners are looking for an appropriate amount of carefully selected and critically assessed reading and will not be at all impressed by a long list of unstructured material. Remember, the most interesting stamp collections are small, focused and thematically-organized with occasional rarities of great value; vast assemblages of random acquisitions are just so many squares of sticky paper.

PRIORITIZING YOUR SEARCH EFFORT

There can be a tendency to be overzealous in searching for literature. There is always the thought in the back of your mind that somewhere out there is a source or reference which everyone else has missed or which will be crucial in validating your hypothesis.

There are undoubtedly cases where fresh researchers have turned up previously unexposed sources, not least because of publication in a foreign language or in an inappropriate journal. If you can find such gems, good luck.

In reality, such highly obscure sources seldom turn out to be as crucial as you might have imagined from their title or context. In such cases you need to decide, as an aspect of good time management and effective working, where your energies are best directed. Spending hours or a fortune tracking down a lost source from 30 years ago, simply to make your collection complete, resembles philately rather than good research. You can probably judge from the work of previous reviewers whether it is worth continuing – will the source really tell you anything new? Knowing when to give up, when to abandon the search, is as important as knowing when to persist.

Box 6.3   The knowledge map

One way of looking at the literature problem is to employ a cartographical metaphor.

Imagine that the totality of mankind's objective (written) knowledge constitutes a map. It is an evolving map of discovery: new regions are constantly being explored, known areas are being charted in ever greater detail and familiar localities are being re-surveyed from new points of view and with better and better instruments.

Parts of the map surface, representing regions known to contain valuable resources or known to be composed of rapidly varying topology, contain a wealth of colour and graphical detail. Increasing the scale of the map in these parts reveals more and more information.

Other areas, where the terrain is either flat and uniform or poorly explored, have much less informational content. Changing the resolution here makes little difference to the map's usefulness.

In trying to review the literature, you have a number of decisions to make and problems to deal with:

☐   to locate the regions of the map which are most appropriate for your study;

☐   to choose the most appropriate scale at which to inspect them;

☐   to try to relate one interesting area with another, even if they do not immediately seem to be contiguous;

☐   to work out whether well-surveyed areas have been properly described or whether a new perspective would be valuable;

☐   to decide whether poorly charted areas are uninteresting or simply unexplored;

☐   to know where the current edges of the map (the limits to current knowledge) are and to decide where you want to set the limits to your inspection of the map.

This sounds like a difficult task. Furthermore, the nature of human knowledge is such that the map might well be three-dimensional rather than flat. Be that as it may, your skill in surveying the literature will be to balance breadth and depth within the material you have available and to do the job with appropriate thoroughness.

If the map metaphor appeals to you, you might want to try applying the mind-mapping technique (Buzan, 1995; see Box 4.3) to your literature survey. Further advice on this approach is also available in Orna and Stevens (1995).

GETTING USEFUL INFORMATION FROM THE LITERATURE

Reading a research paper or any other kind of primary literature source is a skill. It is one of those abilities, like riding a bike or driving a car, which seems hard to acquire at first but which then becomes so easy that you completely forget the effort it once took. This is a problem to watch out for with supervisors: they sometimes seem to imagine that this skill, which they use every day and take for granted, is innate in their students. It will take you a while to get up to speed, so don't be afraid of asking your supervisor to recognize this.

If you are fortunate, the earlier parts of your degree course will have given you some experience in using primary literature sources: much of what follows here may be familiar to you. Nevertheless, reading the literature for your project will probably demand higher rates of coverage and assimilation than you are used to. It would therefore be wise to make sure that you can do it efficiently.

Getting in to any piece of primary literature can be tough. The style may be unfamiliar and the author may have assumed a lot of background knowledge on the part of the reader. It can be especially difficult to overcome the feeling that the paper or article was intended for a small group of 'experts', of which you are not (yet) one, all of whom understand the jargon and can instantly recognize the significance of the work. How do you go about clearing a path through this jungle of information to get to the particular point you are after?

A good approach is to start from the outside, as if you were creeping up on a pride of sleeping lions. Don't move straight in. Take your time, look around and gauge the nature and size of the task. Before trying to extract detailed information, understand the **context** of the work, the **background** of the study and the **reason** why it was carried out. The authors' purpose was probably different, perhaps even quite unconnected, with your own. Work out whether you can expect to gain a set of broad, descriptive notes or a single specific fact. Try to anticipate how much effort you will have to put in: is the information you want likely to be near the surface or deeply buried?

Table 6.1 gives you some hints on using research papers, although you will quickly work out a method for yourself. The structure of this kind of literature varies with discipline, but there are some common key components. Note that you do not have to read **all** of the paper and that, provided you have noted the bibliographic details correctly, you can come back to the paper again later. Be selective in the **order** as well as in the **depth** of reading of each section. It is a good idea to be clear in your mind, before you start, about why you are reading the source and what you want to get out of it (for more on this and the 'SQ3R' approach, see Fairbairn and Winch, 1996).

Table 6.1 Using research papers effectively – what to read, when to read it, what to record				
Order of reading	*Paper section*	*Need to read?*	*Need to record?*	*Value*
1	Title	Essential	Essential	The initial guide content
2	Authors	Essential	Essential	Needed for referencing Remember key/prolific authors Remember where they work
3	Bibliographic details (journal, volume, date, page numbers)	Essential	Essential	Needed for referencing Associate the date with the authors in your mind (say to yourself: 'Smith, 1996')
4	Abstract	Essential	Optional	Guide to content and main findings Read it all. Read the last sentence first
5	First paragraph of Introduction	Optional but wise	Optional	Sets the scene for the work Use as a guide to: ❏ the level at which the paper is set ❏ the authors' writing style ❏ the value of the rest of the Introduction
6	Last paragraph of Discussion	Optional	Optional	The paper's bottom line Often provides a bite-sized summary of the work and its significance
7	Bibliography	Essential	Optional	Use as a source of new references, as described earlier (see page 84)
8	Rest of Introduction	Optional	Optional	Outlines questions being addressed May be a useful review of recent literature
9	Rest of Discussion	Optional	Optional	Skim through, paragraph by paragraph, to find what you need Don't get bogged down in minutiae
10	Results	Optional	Optional	Use the graphics and tables to fix the key results in your mind Read text if this has important details
11	Materials and Methods	Optional	Optional	Usually the most turgid part of the paper Read only if: ❏ you need to understand the detail of the experimental design ❏ you are likely to need this paper's methods yourself ❏ something about the results requires clarification

Skimming can be effective, provided that detail is noted when necessary. Skimming techniques include:

☐ Checking the contents page, if there is one, as a guide to what you might need;
☐ Reading the abstract or summary;
☐ Scanning the headings, sub-headings and any signposts in the margin;
☐ Looking at diagrams and tables, using legends as a source of essential details;
☐ Reading the first and last sentences of each paragraph: this enables you to 'fast forward' through the paragraph when you come to read in depth.

Finally, it is worth remembering that research papers are not intended as works of great literary beauty (although some styles are more pleasant to read than others). They are sources of information and should be treated as such. Use them in the same way as a dictionary or encyclopaedia: find the precise information you want and ignore everything else until you need it.

■ RECORDING BIBLIOGRAPHIC DETAILS

1. WHAT TO RECORD

Your dissertation will contain a bibliography of all the sources you use in researching the information for your project. The information in the bibliography must be complete and correct. These are among the matters of personal integrity upon which others will rely when they come to read your work. Faults in your bibliography are always avoidable, seldom forgivable and invariably marked down heavily by examiners.

Three golden rules for recording what you have read:

1. Do it properly
2. Do it once and once only
3. Do it for every paper you read

In other words, get it right first time. Ensure that you record the information fully and in a form which can be used efficiently when you need it. There are few things more frustrating than trying to find a lost reference or trying to find a paper from misleading or incomplete information. Do it for all papers you read, even the ones you think you may eventually not need.

Table 6.2 provides a checklist of details that you MUST record for every paper or book that you read. In addition, observe the following rules:

- ☐ **Do** be particularly careful of diacritical marks in names and words and make sure, especially for foreign or unusual names, that you have the correct family or surname.
- ☐ **Do** record the details directly from the paper or book, not from the reference which pointed you to it (assume that other authors make mistakes – they often do!)
- ☐ **Don't** correct any apparent errors that you find, for example, in the title – tell it just like it is.
- ☐ **Don't** abbreviate the information you record (for example, by leaving out titles or by substituting *et al.* in place of secondary authors).

Advice on how to refer to your sources in the text of your dissertation is given later (in 'Reference citation' in Chapter 9, page 137) and the Bibliography of this book illustrates how to present the reference details.

The recorded details illustrated in Table 6.2 are three-dimensional: they refer to *origin* (author), *time* (date), and *place* (names and locations). Use the same triangular approach for other types of source material. Your aim must be to record sufficient detail to enable anyone wishing to follow up the reference to do so **quickly, directly** and **unambiguously**. This invariably means including name and date and place. The format of other essential details may need to be adapted to the nature of the source but they must be transparent to an uninformed reader and must not rely on any specialist knowledge or access rights of your own. Remember, you are recording details of the source's location not to prove that you have read it but to enable anyone else to find it.

Another point worth bearing in mind with all source referencing is that the process helps to protect your own academic integrity. As will be pointed out later (in the section 'Accuracy' in Chapter 9, page 127), every statement you make in your dissertation needs to be justified in some way. In the case of statements based on literature and other external sources, providing a reference allows you to transfer responsibility for that information elsewhere. Provided you have: (a) cited or quoted from it accurately and (b) given a complete reference, responsibility for any errors, omissions, fabrications or plagiarisms in the information reverts to the source and not to you. If *your* reference is incomplete or obscure, the buck stops with you.

Table 6.2   Checklist of essential bibliographic details

Type of source (Details needed)   *Example*

Research paper

Author(s)	Meg, M.
Year of publication	1997
Full title of paper	'A statistical analysis of predictive success amongst mystical loterry advisors'
Full journal name	*Journal of Irreproducible Results*
Volume	**3**
Part	2
First and last page numbers	1–49

Book

Authors or editors	Blair, A., Ashdown, P. and Hague, W. (Eds.)
Year of publication	1999
Full title of book	*Chance-based approaches to raising public finance*
Volume (if more than one)	
Edition	2nd
Publisher	Camelot Press
Place of publication	London

Book chapter

All authors: name and all initials	Branson, R.
Year of publication	1999
Full title of paper or chapter	'Non-profit solutions to the management of public games of chance'
First and last page numbers	101–110
Editors: family, name, all initials	Blair, A., Ashdown, P. and Hague, W. (Eds.)
Book title	*Chance-based approaches to raising public finance*
Volume (if more than one)	
Edition	2nd
Publisher	Camelot Press
Place of publication	London

Notes: – Book and journal titles are written in italics
– Volume numbers are in bold
– Give family name and all initials for all authors or editors
– Give the first-listed place of publication if there is more than one

2. HOW TO RECORD

Unless you possess, and can work directly to, a library-friendly laptop computer you will probably have to take your initial bibliographic records by hand. You might want to keep a notebook especially for this.

Alternatively you can photocopy the header page for later reference (but be aware of the disadvantages of photocopying, discussed on page 97). Whatever method you use for this initial record, make sure that you **store** your list of references **electronically**. You don't want to waste time keying in bibliographic information more than once, so keep it in a form which you can use easily later on.

There are several options:

1.   as an ordinary word-processor text file;
2.   as a database (or spreadsheet) file, using the items in the checklist (Table 6.2) as category/column names; or
3.   as a bibliographic software file.

The first option has the advantage of simplicity and will give you the information in the correct form at writing-up time. Its disadvantage (depending on your word-processor and your familiarity with its more esoteric features) is the ease with which you can order and sort the references. Databases and spreadsheets are easy to use and make sorting and ordering a doddle. However, you must give sufficient thought to the design of the table right at the outset. Make sure you can enter and retrieve data easily, and avoid setting any constraints, such as field data types or character limits, which might require you to compromise any information which is in an unusual format.

For option 3 in the above list, several types of bibliographic software are available although some are expensive and more elaborate than you need. Their advantage is that they prompt you for the appropriate information at input and allow you to produce an output in any required style. They also have good searching facilities (you can create a keyword list) and may have ways of preventing errors such as duplication or missing page numbers. They can be set up to import data directly from on-line search engines, thereby saving you from having to type in any information at all. They can also be integrated with the more common word-processors; this allows you to include references from your bibliography directly in your text at writing-up time and generating a complete, ready-made bibliography when you have finished. As you might imagine, the use of these features, even in the most user-friendly software, requires practice.

Before committing yourself to option 2 or option 3, make sure that you know how to retrieve the information into your word-processor – don't be stuck with incompatible files or software which is too complicated to use. And finally...

As with all electronic data, **don't keep a back-up file. Keep two**.

RECORDING INFORMATION FROM LITERATURE

1. WHAT TO RECORD

As well as compiling a list of material you have read for your bibliography, you will want to make notes on its content. To decide what to record, you need to be clear in your mind **why** you are reading that particular source. It is worth spending a moment or two thinking about the answer to this question when you start to read your paper or article and to continue thinking critically about it as you go.

Here are some of the reasons why you might be consulting a particular item of literature:

❑ as a means of filling in background information;
❑ as a way of reviewing current opinions in an area of knowledge;
❑ to follow the logic of an explanation or hypothesis;
❑ to provide material for a case study;
❑ to enable you to cite a particular body of evidence;
❑ to obtain a specific quotation;
❑ as a source of specific pieces of data;
❑ to find details about a particular type of experimental design or analysis;
❑ to obtain details of a technique you wish to use.

Your aim in making notes should be to avoid, as far as possible, having to read that particular source again at some time in the future. Ideally, the only legitimate reason for re-reading should be that your own perspective or informational needs have changed. The notes you make now can help you to decide in the future whether this particular item would be worth looking at again.

As well as jotting down the key facts contained in the source, you might want to note down some of the following:

❑ where you obtained the reference to this source; this helps to jog the memory and place information in context;
❑ how this source relates to others ('Follows from Sellers, 1980', 'Repeats Reeves *et al.*, 1997', 'Disagrees with Mortimer *et al.*, 1996', etc.);
❑ your current opinion of how useful the source is ('Informative', 'Speculative', 'Critical', 'Detailed', 'Rubbish', etc.);
❑ key extracts from a table or a sketch of graphical data;
❑ methodological details.

Keep your notes **short** but **meaningful** and make sure that you will be able to understand them again in several months time. Invent a shorthand to save time and space, but be consistent and don't make it too obscure. Avoid signs and symbols which may lose their meaning once the context of the reading is lost.

2. HOW TO RECORD

The advice earlier was to put bibliographic details directly into electronic format. This is unlikely to be the best way to deal with your initial informational notes, however. Paper is flexible stuff which can be cut, scribbled on, spread around, piled up, carried about in individual pieces, or even scrunched to a ball in fury. You can do very few of these exciting things with a computer. Compared with written script, the amount of text visible on a computer screen at any one time is limited and generally linear in the way it flows. Spontaneous freehand sketches to show how ideas are related come naturally when you have a pen in your hand but are a pain on the keyboard. In short, paper offers you the utmost freedom and flexibility; it is the medium of choice for your primary note-taking.

One of the best ways of recording nuggets of literature remains the good old-fashioned **file card**. This ancient bibliographic device is far from trendy but it is simple, fun, flexible and, to many researchers, indispensable. Buy a couple of large packets of the A6 size and get a sturdy box to stack them in. Take a half-dozen or so with you in an envelope whenever you go to the library or consult the archives. Use one per article or source, setting aside the top couple of lines for the bibliographic details. Number them sequentially in a top corner. The rest of the card is for making notes in any way you choose.

When you get back to your computer, you can quickly plough through the cards one by one, turning the bibliographic details into electrons once and for all. **Then** treat the cards as malleable nuggets of information. Sort them in any order you choose: by author, by date, by subject, by origin or according to any other whimsical criterion which has meaning for you. You could label some envelopes and use them to group your cards according to the ideas they refer to. Pull out ones which need more work. Tear up ones which make no sense. From time to time, make yourself feel better by throwing the whole lot out on the desk and reordering them. Pin important ones above your bed and stare at them before going to sleep. Use them as information currency with friends if you are working in a group. And finally, when you start to write your literature review, you'll have a ready-made set of cue cards in your hand.

3. PHOTOCOPYING

It can be very tempting to avoid the chore of note-taking by photocopying the papers and articles you need. Photocopying is brilliant technology but it is not always a good idea. Apart from being expensive and wasteful of trees, it can be positively disadvantageous to knowledge and understanding. Note-taking doesn't just create a record of what you have read, it helps you to digest the information (Box 6.4). Having a photocopy in your hand can give you a false sense of security – it can leave you with the mistaken feeling that you have dealt adequately with that particular item (ticked it off the list) when in fact all you have done is avoided the key facts and piled up yet more material for later study.

Box 6.4   Recording and interpretation: the digital parrot

In the following quotation, the Nobel Prize-winning journalist Gabriel Garcia Márquez discusses the effect of the tape recorder on journalism. If the subject is appropriate to your specific project or interests, read the quotation literally. If not, try substituting 'photocopier' for 'recorder', 'researcher' for 'journalist', and 'literature source' for 'interlocutor' and 'interviewee'.

> Somebody needs to teach young reporters that the recorder is not a substitute for memory, but a simple evolved version of the serviceable, old-fashioned notebook.
> The tape recorder listens, repeats – like a digital parrot – but it does not think. It is loyal but it does not have a heart; and, in the end, the literal version it will have captured will never be as trustworthy as that kept by the journalist who pays attention to the real words of the interlocutor and, at the same time, evaluates and qualifies them from his knowledge and experience.
> The tape recorder is entirely to blame for the undue importance now attached to the interview ... Now even the print media seems to share the erroneous idea that the voice of truth is not that of the journalist but that of the interviewee. Maybe the solution is to return to the lowly notebook so the journalist can edit as he listens, and relegate the tape recorder to its real role as invaluable witness.

Márquez, G.G. (1997) 'Hacks in the time of tape recorders'; Speech to Inter-American Press Association, quoted in *The Observer*, 25 May, 1997.

Photocopying has its place in the following circumstances:

❑   you are in a distant library, or one with limited access, and need to grab a bunch of references for later study in your own time;

❐   the article has many references that you will want to follow up, and writing them all down would be a waste of time;

❐   you need to be sure that a quotation has been made and cited exactly;

❐   you find this the best way of temporarily holding bibliographic details prior to electronic storage;

❐   you anticipate needing to refer again and again to a particular illustration, item of data or method;

❐   you find it helpful to underline key material or make annotations on the page.

Even then, it may only be necessary to copy particular pages. If you do choose to do this, it is always wise to copy the header page as well so that you don't lose track of where the material came from. Usually, the header page contains the abstract as a bonus.

DOS AND DON'TS OF READING THE LITERATURE

❐   **Do** take bibliographic details once and once only

❐   **Do** make notes on what you have read

❐   **Don't** record or quote what you haven't read yourself

❐   **Don't** mistake photocopying for reading and assimilation

CHAPTER

7

MAKING PROGRESS

 ## HANDLING YOUR SUPERVISOR

Your supervisor is going to be one of the most important and useful people in your life for the next few months and you need to cultivate a good relationship. It is very likely that, prior to thinking about your project, your only meetings were confined to more or less formal teaching situations. Your attitude towards him or her, in so far as you had one, was probably a combination of respect, awe, calculated deference, fear, contempt, indifference or even dislike and hate, or any of the other complex emotions of human interaction.

But from now on you will need to have a relationship which works to your benefit. Undoubtedly the best approach is to aim for a relationship of **amicable professionalism**. This requires some self-confidence on your part and some adaptability on your supervisor's. As a student, it can be difficult to get away from the feeling that your supervisor, like any other member of academic staff, is constantly in judgement mode. It is equally difficult, sometimes, for academics to avoid a judgemental posture. Maybe that is inevitable – after all, in the end he or she will have to judge your performance and give you a mark for your work. But there is a great deal of room for manoeuvre beyond that side of the relationship, room for you to get on well together and for you both to gain from the experience.

Table 7.1 suggests some attitudes and behaviours conducive to amicable professionalism. It amounts to a kind of contract since it involves effort and agreement on both sides. Some institutions encourage students and supervisors to draw up formal contracts defining roles and responsibilities. There may be a departmental statement for you to sign which establishes the working relationship and specifies things like the frequency of meetings, the pattern of work and the kinds of advice which your supervisor is expected to give. This can be especially valuable if your supervisor will be involved in the final assessment of your work, helping to clarify the sometimes hazy borders between guidance and assistance and between advice and help. It will also create a framework for formal procedures if things go wrong.

Table 7.1 The student–supervisor relationship: amicable professionalism	
Student's attitude to supervisor	*Supervisor's attitude to student*
Acknowledge greater knowledge and experience	Acknowledge the need to learn
Accept advice	Offer constructive advice
Show increasing independence as the work proceeds	Give support and encouragement
Avoid being defensive in the face of criticism	Give objective criticism
Respect existing work practices and conventions	Provide a safe and secure working environment
Don't waste resources	Provide appropriate resources
Respond to communication and keep appointments	Respond quickly and fully to requests for help
Don't hide unresolved problems	Anticipate problems as far as possible
Recognise when help is provided	Deal with problems rapidly
Complete planned work on time	Moderate and return work swiftly
Use research time as effectively as possible	Acknowledge time limitations
Take responsibility for the work schedule	Give space for reflection as well as learning
Use imagination but recognize limits	Encourage inquisitiveness but set boundaries
Be frank and honest about progress	Encourage and recognize success
Don't be afraid to ask stupid questions	Answer all questions fairly and fully
Invite friendship but respect its limits	Encourage friendship but respect it limits
Seek support when considering jobs and careers	Freely offer career advice and act as referee

KNOW WHO YOUR SUPERVISOR IS

The person who has ultimate **academic** responsibility for you may not be the person with whom you work most closely on your project. Any one of the following members of the department may be given the task of discussing project details with you, looking after you and giving you day-to-day guidance on the job:

❑ *Research fellow*
  A professional researcher, probably with a PhD, who is either permanently employed in the department, engaged on a short-term (a number of years) contract, or visiting from another institution.
❑ *Research assistant*
  Either a post-doctoral researcher ('post-doc'; has a PhD) or a graduate (has a Bachelor's degree); may be working concurrently for a PhD, usually on a limited term contract.
❑ *Technician*
  May be either a permanent member of department staff or attached to a research programme on a limited contract.
❑ *Postgraduate student*
  A research student with a Bachelor's degree working full-time towards a PhD, probably over three to four years.

Alternatively, you may have to spend some time away from the department working with someone who has no direct connection with your university at all.

These arrangements will have been made with good reason: the person you are asked to work with will have some particular expertise, experience, knowledge or facilities which you need. You may come to regard this person as your guide, mentor and friend and they may well be the one who ends up knowing most about you and your work. Their opinion of your progress will almost certainly be sought at assessment time.

Nevertheless, it is essential to realize that this person is unable to assume **academic responsibility** for your studies. If things don't go quite according to plan, for example, they and you are answerable not to one another but to the academic faculty member who has you on his or her list of students. Similarly, you should know whom to refer to if you get conflicting advice: all the people you work with will have their own opinions about how the work should be carried out or how a particular result should be interpreted. There is great potential here for significant wastage of your time and effort, so be selfish and don't let such differences fester.

So the bottom line is, make sure you are clear about who, in the final analysis, your supervisor really is. Make a point of talking to your real supervisor regularly and keep him or her fully informed about your progress. Give them copies of any research plans or interim reports you write. The fact that they assigned you to someone else and may have little direct advice to give you themselves does not imply any lack of interest in or concern for your progress.

MEETINGS AND ACTION PLANS

Finding the best way of getting the most out of your meetings with your supervisor depends a great deal on the nature of the subject you are studying. It also depends on the organization of the department and on practical features such as workloads, timetables and locations. What you are after from your supervisor is **quality time**.

From your supervisor's point of view, quality time probably means an uninterrupted meeting which starts punctually and gets down to useful work straight away. You can help this process by making sure that you arrive well-prepared for the meeting and armed with all the information you might need. It also helps if you have already thought about and formulated the questions you want to ask or already had a go at analysing the data you need help with.

From your point of view, you want to come away from the meeting feeling that you have learned something. You will want to be sure about what your next step is going to be and to have a clear view of what you have to get done before the next meeting.

Whatever your relationship with your supervisor, it is wise to keep some record of the meeting (see 'Keep a project diary' in Chapter 8, page 114). This will not only enable you to remind yourself of the outcome, it will enable you to remind your supervisor, next time you meet, of where your discussions had got to. If it is your supervisor's habit to scribble down notes and diagrams during the meeting, ask to save them as a reminder of what was discussed. These fleeting scraps of wisdom may be of lasting value to you but will be destined for the bin if you don't claim them.

Some supervisors like to use action plans. An action plan is an agreed statement, perhaps recorded in a project diary, which summarizes where you have got to since the last meeting, what you talked about at this meeting and where you plan to be by the time of the next one. The formality of the statement will be a matter for agreement between the two of you, although there are departments which set guidelines of good practice as part of the teaching quality assurance process. You might be asked to record the following details at the end of each meeting:

❐   Date of meeting
❐   Summary of action since last meeting
❐   Summary of current work in progress
❐   Any current difficulties or threats to progress
❐   Agreed goals for the next week (fortnight, month, etc.)
❐   Date and time of next meeting

Whatever you do, look upon the action plan as a positive contribution to progress review, not as a chore or (worst of all) as a disincentive to asking your supervisor for help. If your supervisor doesn't suggest an action plan but you think it might be helpful, make the suggestion yourself.

Finally on this point, don't be surprised if from time to time your supervisor asks for **your** opinion or advice. Once you start to get to grips with your subject and have your own opinions about it, your supervisor may see you as a useful sounding-box for his or her own latest ideas. This is flattering, of course, but reflects the fact that you are on similar wavelengths and thinking about similar problems. Your relatively recent critical assessment of literature may mean that you are able to offer precisely the fresh, uncomplicated opinions which he or she is looking for.

WHAT TO DO IF THE RELATIONSHIP STARTS TO BREAK DOWN

Personal relationships in any walk of life seldom run smoothly and your relationship with your supervisor will be no exception. There will be times when you find it difficult to talk to one another and you may even fall out completely. Because of the academic/judgemental component of the relationship, falling out mostly takes the form of silence or avoidance rather than an actual row.

You may feel, for example, that you want to ignore advice and press ahead on your own. Alternatively, you may want to move away completely from deep involvement in the work. You might feel that you are getting less than adequate support from your supervisor or that your work is of poor standard and likely to attract criticism.

These and similar feelings are signs that something is wrong. They will not be resolved by time. Do something about them as soon as possible:

❑ Talk to your **supervisor**, if at all possible, recognizing the problem frankly. It will soon become clear whether the problem originates within the work or from the personalities involved. As with bank managers, it's best to talk to them earlier rather than later. Work can often be reconsidered and then restructured or altered to improve the atmosphere. Personalities are more tricky to change, but it is worth having a go.

❑ You might be able to achieve an understanding or a *modus operandi* which, though less than perfect, enables the work to continue productively. Although it helps to get on well with your supervisor, this is not obligatory. It is quite acceptable to emphasize the professional rather than the amicable side of the relationship; exclude the latter completely if that is the way that works best for you.

❑ For a more serious breakdown you need to get help elsewhere. Your **personal tutor** should be able to help, firstly by giving you time to think and listening to what you have to say, but also by sorting out practical difficulties. It is well worth keeping in touch with your tutor even if your supervisor becomes your new focus for personal support. Your tutor probably knows the department well and can reach parts of it to which you have no access. He or she will have a professional relationship with your supervisor which means that they can discuss what is going on from an entirely different, impersonal angle. This can work greatly to your advantage and should not be seen as in any way threatening. Your tutor will not take sides but may be able to get rapidly to the root of the problem, in a manner not available to you, and do something about it.

❑ If the storm is very severe, your next source of shelter must be the **head of department**. Heads of department take the ultimate academic responsibility for the progress of students. They like a quiet life and a harmonious department and are therefore keen to resolve rather than exacerbate problems. Despite the exalted title, your head of department is available to you and you can expect to receive just as much objectivity and confidentiality as you would get from any other member of staff.

❑ Don't forget the other advice and **support services** which your university provides. Information on these is readily available. The university counsellor may not have a clue about the subject of your degree, let alone that of your project, but you can guarantee that he or she will have an expert appreciation of what makes people tick and a willingness to listen.

Whatever type of help you seek, try to be objective and constructive about the problem and avoid personal criticism. If you perceive that things are going badly wrong, to the point where you might start to seek some kind of academic redress, it will help if you have documented the problem. This would be one reason for keeping a diary of your project work, although of course you should not be keeping it primarily for this purpose.

GIVING FEEDBACK TO YOUR SUPERVISOR

Towards the end of your project work, don't be afraid to tell your supervisor, politely of course, what you thought of the supervision you received. Feedback from students is a common feature of formal course and module review and is equally valuable for project work. Some departments have a formal recording process for student comment and you should make full use of such opportunities. A culture of constructive feedback makes a useful contribution to the maintenance of high standards and effective work. You will undoubtedly have benefited from the comments of earlier students. Keep the chain of benefit going by having your say.

Sometimes, groups of students working in a similar field or under a single supervisor are encouraged to form consortia with the aim of conferring among themselves about the supervisor's performance. Such groups may meet at regular intervals during the project period and give regular feedback. Some students feel more comfortable with the slightly greater anonymity which this system affords for their comments.

However you do it, your supervisor will relish praise if things went well but will be strong enough to take any criticisms you may have, provided that they are given in a reasonably objective and constructive way.

SUPERVISOR AS PERSONAL TUTOR

If you are fortunate, your relationship with your supervisor will be harmonious and productive. Depending on the arrangements in your department, you may well get to see your supervisor frequently as well as regularly. You will get to know each other quite well, perhaps, to the extent that your supervisor takes over some of the personal support role previously played by your tutor. This is fine – universities want their students to be helped and supported in the most appropriate way for them.

It would be wise, however, if this starts to happen, to keep in touch with your tutor and let him or her know what is going on. Your tutor still needs to know that your studies are going well, that you are happy and confident and that the reduction in the number of your visits has no negative connotations.

RELATING TO THE DEPARTMENT

Privileges

The relationship between you and your supervisor has a wider context which you should be aware of. For the duration of your project you will become an active contributor to the total research effort of the department. It may seem that your project is simply an educational exercise being carried out largely for your benefit, but in fact it will have a direct relationship with other work which your supervisor, his or her research group or the departmental team is doing. Because of this, it provides a unique opportunity for finding out at first hand how an academic department operates, who does what, who answers to whom and how the whole ship stays afloat and on course. No amount of lectures, seminars, tutorials or computer-aided learning can possibly give you this insight.

Responsibilities

Like all privileges, this one has several attendant responsibilities. For example, you will need to respect the personal space of others working in the same laboratory/office/workshop. 'They' are likely to be a varied bunch of folk including other undergraduate students, postgraduates, research assistants, technicians, post-doctoral fellows, academic staff and visiting professors. Like any social group, they will have developed a hierarchy (which may take some time for you to discern) and will depend upon each other's individual skills and knowledge. You may have to learn and fit in with their written or unwritten rules and rotas about who does the chores (washing glassware, refilling the photocopier, reordering consumables, answering the telephone), when and how often. There may be a set of shared information (for example, quality control data on a routine method) to which you find yourself contributing on a regular basis and which is trusted by the whole group. You will need to appreciate which bits of kit are communally available and which are for personal use only. Indeed, you will need to carve out your own personal space adjacent to theirs and fill it with your own collection of artefacts.

It can be great fun working in this kind of environment and enduring friendships can be forged. You must be aware, however, that you are entering their niche and that their work needs to proceed in spite of rather than because of your presence. This is not too difficult if you treat your new colleagues with courtesy and respect. On the whole, you will find the people you have to work with very willing to help and answer your dumb questions. They may even be prepared to answer them more than once! Don't be afraid to ask. Universities are places of shared knowledge and the culture of mutual learning reaches well beyond the artificial formalities of the lecture theatre.

Personal attitudes

Adopting the right personal attitude can go a long way to making the group environment a harmonious one. Academic departments typically have a high turnover of personnel for one reason or another, and there may be elusive individuals who are talked about but rarely seen. Group banter, sometimes aggressive, sometimes malicious, will occur. Your best bet is to ignore the gossip, avoid taking sides and be as pleasant as you can to everyone. It is worth remembering that *all* the people around you have their own opinions, relationships, gripes, uncertainties, personal problems and insecurities. But unlike you, they live out the whole of their working life in this environment.

If you are very unfortunate, you may find yourself having to work closely with someone whose views, behaviour or personal habits you find particularly offensive or intolerable. You supervisor is your best recourse in this situation and you must talk about your difficulties rather than let them become prejudicial to your work. The earlier advice about trying to remain constructive and objective about things also applies here, although there are limits to tolerance even for those approaching sainthood. Working with others and taking part in departmental life will be a challenge and will stretch your patience, but you should never have to put up with any kind of abuse or deliberate misconduct.

Other opportunities

Working within the department in this way offers you several new opportunities. Here are some you might want to take advantage of:

❏   Go to departmental research seminars. Go, even if the title of the talk means little to you. Listen carefully, take notes and try to understand what is being described. If you feel able, ask a question about something you did not follow. Don't be intimidated by the age, seniority or apparently greater knowledge of the rest of the audience – your academic mentors will be impressed simply by the fact that you raised your hand and gave voice in public. And who knows, you might be asking the very question they were too embarrassed to ask themselves.

❏   Talk to postgraduate students in the department about their work and try to appreciate its place in the greater scheme of things. These people are likely to be closer to your age and recent experience than anyone else around. Besides asking about the nitty-gritty of their research work, find out if they did their undergraduate studies here or at another university. What made them move/remain? Ask them about their career aspirations, about why they decided to do further research work, about where their sponsorship comes from and about the tricks they employ to survive on a subsistence wage.

❏   Find out about the conferences which people in the department are going to. If the department suddenly seems to be evacuated for a week in early summer, it's likely that some big, regular event in the research calendar is taking place. If you can get to it yourself, that's an added bonus. If not, when they return ask to see the programme and abstracts of presented papers.

❏   Exploit any opportunities to contact representatives of industry or large employers who might be visiting. Look out for sales demonstrations or exhibitions of new equipment within the department. Keep your ear to the ground and ask your supervisor to introduce you to visitors if you think it might be useful. You will make lots of mistakes and follow many loose trails but you will make yourself streetwise in the process. Provided you are polite, there is no harm in raising your profile.

◼ MAINTAINING SANITY

Project work is tough. It offers you intellectual freedom but when coupled with the self-motivation and commitment expected of you, this can be frightening.

For day-to-day advice on progress and motivation you should be able talk to your supervisor. This is particularly important when timing starts to go astray or if you feel that you are beginning to lose the plot. Look upon this as a progress review rather than a sign of any sort of weakness or failure on your part. He or she will also have been thinking about whether the work is going according to plan and might even be grateful that you have been the first one to mention it. Your supervisor will either offer reassurance (which you should treat as genuine and accept) or suggest practical ways of rescheduling the work and getting back on course.

Sometimes, however, uncertainties develop which are less easy to describe and which you may feel uneasy about relating to your supervisor. You might experience some of these feelings:

- 'I don't know whether this is what I really want to do.'
- 'Am I putting in the right amount of effort?'
- 'Is the work going as well as it should?'
- 'Will I get it finished in time?'
- 'My results don't mean very much.'
- 'All my friends have got their results already.'
- 'I haven't had time to read all the literature yet.'
- 'The work seems tedious and boring.'
- 'I never seem to feel on top of my work these days.'
- 'My supervisor never tells me what he or she really thinks about my work.'
- 'All my ideas seem like commonsense – are they really new?'

It would be patronizing to say that these uncertainties are unimportant. They are real enough and they need to be given attention. On the other hand, it would also be fair to say that many of these feelings are engendered by the nature of the work. Research is a lonely business, precisely because it has no certain outcome. Insecurity goes with the territory. If it is any comfort, you are in good company: most of the people you see around you also feel this way.

No one knows the antidote to these feelings, so what you have to do is live through them. In other words, you have to maintain your sanity in the face of pressure.

You will develop your own ways of dealing with the pressure. One way is to use a sanity maintenance chart (Table 7.2). Another is to make use of help from friends, colleagues and academic staff. You could identify for yourself an unofficial hit list of people you trust and to whom you can turn when things get tough (Box 7.1).

These approaches will not make the feelings go away but they will increase your chance of surviving unscathed. The keyword here really is *survival*. Academic life at this level is challenging: you need to adapt to survive and succeed. Work at it for yourself and try to maintain your self-confidence, but let others know how you feel.

| Table 7.2   Sanity maintenance chart |

To be used daily, weekly or as needed.
Instructions for use:
1.   Do one thing from each column.
2.   Add something new to each column.

Productive things to do	Interactive things to do	Diversions
Make lists of things to do	Talk to a friend	Read a slushy novel
Rewrite your CV	Talk to your tutor	Go for a walk in the rain
Write up your project diary	Phone home	Surf the Net
Change your work routine	Say hello to your cleaner	Plan a holiday
Reorganize your reference list	Email an old school friend	Spring clean your hard drive
Do some job hunting	Write a letter	Clean your shoes
Draw a mind map	Join the Rag committee	Mend your bike tyre

RETAINING PERSPECTIVE

The other threat to your sanity comes from the commitment you are expected to show. To carry out your project you have to set your mind's eye on a very short focus. The aperture is narrow and it's difficult to let enough light in. Your work is so intense and specific, so wrapped up in its own terminology and methodology, that you probably have difficulty in explaining what you are doing to anyone outside a small, charmed circle of fellow students.

It's as well to remember from time to time just how narrow your project studies are. They need to be narrow, but they need not make the rest of your life narrow as well.

Box 7.1   Your personal hit list

Make a list of people you can turn to when you feel in need of help or support. Your hit list might include:

❏   someone who makes good coffee and will do so at unsociable hours;
❏   someone outside your academic life who you can visit or 'phone unexpectedly for a chat;
❏   someone who enjoys a good mutual moan at the system, the university, the staff and anyone/anything else in the firing line;
❏   someone who will listen disinterestedly but not uninterestedly to your wild ideas;
❏   someone who will reinforce your view that you are working too hard;
❏   someone who will tell you it's OK to do something you feel strongly about;
❏   someone who will tell you it's OK not to do something you feel unsure about;
❏   someone who will wait for you while you go for a difficult meeting with your supervisor;
❏   someone who will save a late place for you in the lunch queue.

The chances are you will find yourself offering the same service to these people in return.

Box 7.2 has a refocusing exercise to help you change the focus once you have started work on your project. It will help to broaden the aperture and refresh the perspective when the cloud of obscurity threatens. You can add this to the sanity maintenance chart (Table 7.2) under 'Productive things to do'. Don't put it in the 'diversions' column – as well as giving your brain an overhaul, it actually generates useful material for your project.

Box 7.2   Refocusing exercise

1.   Open up a new, blank document on your word-processor.

2.   Think of someone in your family whom you like to talk to, someone who knows you well but has no knowledge of the subject you are studying at university. It would be even better if they never went to university themselves. We'll call him Uncle Ebenezer.

3.   Start a letter: '*Dear Uncle Ebenezer, I thought you would like to hear what I am doing at university. I'm working on my research project just at the moment and it's getting really interesting.*'

4.   Tell Uncle Eb what your project is all about. Imagine the old charmer picking your letter up from the door mat and settling down at the kitchen table with a packet of Hob-Nobs to read what you have to

Box 7.2   Continued

say. Start by giving him the title of your project. To avoid him choking on biscuit crumbs you'll need to jot a few definitions down so that he knows what the title means. (Remember, you are trying to inform him, not flatter yourself – he knows you far too well to be impressed by long words.)

5.   Run a few lines of background past him, so that he gets the picture. Is he really starting to understand what it's all about? Perhaps you need to use an analogy with something that is familiar to him. Or perhaps you can connect it with something he might have read in the papers or seen on telly. Make it relevant to him. Put it in words that he can understand.

6.   You'll have to keep stopping and explaining things that he might not have followed, but don't worry about the order in which your thoughts appear. Get the information down one way or another and use the cut and paste feature of your word-processor to cover your tracks later on. (The invention of the word-processor has transformed the art of letter writing!)

7.   Now that you are some way down the screen, and Uncle Eb is already on his third tea bag, it's time to wrap the story up. Round things off with a word or two about where you have currently got to in your work and what the next task is.

8.   Finish the letter with a final sentence or two of pleasantries: '*I hope you understood all this. I must go now as I have a tutorial to prepare for. I would love to hear how your dahlias are doing – will your blooms win the village show again this year? Lots of love from . . .*'

9.   Now, highlight and delete the start and end of your letter (the bits in italics, steps 3 and 8). Save the file, on the disk you use for your project, under the following filename 'SUMMARY1.TXT'. Forget all about it for now – you will stumble across it (and its successors, SUMMARY2.TXT, SUMMARY3.TXT . . .) when writing-up time comes.

SOME BRIGHT IDEAS

 ## KEEP AN IDEAS BOOK

Keep a small notebook in which to jot down ideas about your project as you go along. The things you write can be the kind of 'life, the universe and everything' ideas which jump at you in the middle of the night, or more prosaic bits and pieces such as a new search keyword to try or the molecular weight of the particular hydrate of sodium dihydrogen phosphate you need for your buffer. You can make a note of potential connections between ideas that you might want to think more deeply about later on or interesting but peripheral observations made during your work which don't seem to fit within the formal record-keeping process.

The point about this book is that it has *no* order, *no* organization, *no* discipline. Because its information is unfiltered and uncatalogued, no decision has to be made about how, where or when to make an entry. You find things in it by turning the pages and remembering where to look. The items you pass on the way get burned into the mind and start to shape the grander and more coherent thoughts which you need to marshal at writing-up time.

Carry the ideas book with you at all times, sleep with it, and don't let anyone else see it. Keep it anxiety-free. It will become a constant source of reassurance and a reminder of transient thoughts. By the time you come to write your project up, you may be surprised to find that the ideas book contains all you need.

KEEP A PROJECT DIARY

A diary is a boring but useful document. Its purpose and function are completely different from that of an ideas book. A diary has inherent order and generates its own, nagging empty spaces as the days go by. Keeping it up to date demands a certain kind of self-discipline. The best way of keeping a project diary is to record on a daily or (maximum) weekly basis all your project-related activities. Whether you record events or thoughts or both is up to you. The essential point is that you have a traceable record of how your work progressed. All kinds of information, even quite complex facts and ideas, are easier to remember if you can associate them with timed events or stages of progress.

Important things to put in your research project diary include the dates and outcomes of chats with your supervisor, dates when you did particular pieces of practical work, occasions when you felt you were moving deliberately from one stage of the work to another, records of ephemeral events such as 'phone calls or informal discussions over a beer, dates when you found out especially important information, details of research seminars you attended.

Your diary will have many uses. For example, it will:

❐   become a valuable tool in the reflection and time management processes, described earlier;
❐   help you to hold constructive conversations with your supervisor based on goals and achievements rather than hopes and regrets;
❐   provide a mass of progress-related details at writing-up time which you never thought you would need.

Sometimes project diaries are marked as part of the formal assessment procedure. Of course, you will be told if you are expected to maintain one for this purpose.

WRITE UP AS YOU GO ALONG

This particularly applies to methodological details and steps in the analysis of data. It goes without saying that meticulous record-keeping is a prerequisite for success in any kind of empirical study but the *exact* relationship between your lab book or field notes and the final, written description of your methods in the dissertation may not be all that obvious. Furthermore, when it comes to writing up this section for real, the prospect of transcribing that mass of disorganized, prosaic detail can be a depressing one.

The tip here is to build up your methods section as you go along. In other words, try committing the procedural record directly to disk in tiny chunks and at regular intervals. The precise form in which you do this is not too important, at least at the beginning. You will find that you soon adopt a convenient style and that there are large sections which can be short-circuited by judicious use of the cut and paste feature of your word-processor.

Finally, when you do have to get it all into the proper format for presentation, all you should have to do is rearrange existing material, check out details and tie off loose ends.

 ## BECOME A WORDSMITH

You probably don't think of yourself as a 'writer' (one of the kind who populate the denser sections of the Sunday newspapers!) but you will need to be able to write if your dissertation is to be anywhere near readable. Why not become a wordsmith instead? It's as easy as 1, 2, 3, needs no new tools, and the training comes in three easy stages:

Stage 1
Accept the following statements:

- ❏ Your ability to type accurately and fast is limited (but improving!)
- ❏ You never write quite what you mean the first time ~~round~~ through.
- ❏ You could probably ~~say what you mean to say more concisely~~ use fewer words if they were chosen more skilfully.

Stage 2
Write something on the word-processor (a paragraph at a time is the right amount) as rapidly as possible and as carelessly as it comes.

Stage 3
Combine the following into *one* process instead of three separate and sequential ones:

- ❏ Correct your typos.
- ❏ Think about what you have written.
- ❏ Reduce the length of the paragraph.

If, like most of us, you normally write in a haphazard way you will find this hard and confusing at first (especially Stage 3!). After a bit of practice, however, you will realize that words and meanings are really so closely intertwined that correction, adjustment and improvement can be treated as one and the same process. The result will be polished prose with fewer mistakes, written in less time.

Remember this:

> People who choose their words carefully usually have something important to say.

■ NEVER THROW ANYTHING AWAY

This goes against your mother's advice, but she need never know. Keep a box file, a shoebox, a bucket or some other capacious storage device for lodging used bits of paper. Whenever you write or rewrite anything, put the original in this container rather than the rubbish bin. It's also a good place to put rejected file cards, old sheets of raw data, unwanted sketches and plans or obsolete notes of meetings and interviews. Look upon this as a halfway house towards disposal from which accidentally discarded gems can be retrieved.

You can do a similar thing with unwanted chunks of electronic text or data. Keep a file on your disk labelled 'Dump' or 'Extras' or 'O&S' (odds & sods) into which you can deposit all those bits and pieces which don't seem to fit anywhere but which might, just might come in useful someday.

Towards the end of your project work, have a trawl through your box and check that nothing of importance has been missed. You will find it refreshing, instructive and flattering to see how your ideas, skills and level of understanding have developed since you started. The various strata of the box or disk will amount to an archaeological record of your work from which a valuable historical perspective can be gleaned.

Chuck the lot in a recycling bin the moment your dissertation has been finally handed in.

■ SAVE SOME CHOCOLATE FOR BREAKFAST

There will be some parts of your project work that you look forward to working on, but many others which you find unappealing, worrying or just a chore. It could be, for example, that you enjoy the mechanical process of tabulating the day's survey results but find the prospect of sitting down and starting the analysis so bothersome ('Will it show anything useful?') that you can invariably find other things to do instead. Similarly, you might have been putting off the writing of a particular part of the dissertation because you are uncertain about how to express what you want to say or unclear about where your ideas are leading.

In these cases it helps enormously if you can organize your work in such a way that **you look forward** to whatever is coming next. In other words, you want to arrange tasks so that you have a positive, optimistic feeling towards the next thing on the list.

One way to do this is to leave pleasant jobs *unfinished*, at least temporarily. For example, you could deliberately leave the final part of the tabulation incomplete before you go off to lunch so that you can look forward to rounding it off when you return (and then, of course, going straight into the analysis). And similarly, it is much more pleasant to go to bed knowing that there are just a few easy sentences to be tidied up first thing tomorrow than to lie awake worrying how you are going to start that awful last chapter when dawn comes.

So, if this is your kind of problem, try taking a break just before you have completed a pleasant task. Give yourself the treat of hitting the ground running next time. It's a cheap trick to play on yourself, but it works.

■ DIVIDE YOUR DAY

Here's another very simple time management idea which might help if you are having trouble organizing your life. It is especially useful if you are suddenly faced with free periods of time which you know you should be using for study but which lack the imposed structure of external obligations such as lectures. Good examples are vacations, end-of-semester weeks and days set aside for writing up the dissertation.

Divide each day into thirds: morning, afternoon and evening. Make up your mind to devote two of them to study. The remaining third is for you to do whatever you like with (but it must include the household chores as well as social and pleasurable things).

The order of the thirds doesn't matter and need not be the same each day. It's up to you to be honest with yourself in setting the starting and finishing times of each third and in making sure that they are of similar lengths. It is also important to be totally single-minded once a study third has begun: avoid truncating or extending one third and trying to compensating for it in another – that's a recipe for confusion and the collapse of all your good intentions.

That's all there is to it. If you can keep it up over a significant period of time then both sanity and productivity, not to mention a glowing feeling of self-righteousness, are guaranteed.

BE OPTIMISTIC

Set yourself realistic goals and targets for your work but do so in the grand and positive expectation that you will achieve them. When you reflect on your progress, pick out the ideas which worked and the jobs which got finished rather than the stuff which fell by the wayside. If you are worried that this approach is a recipe for continual disappointment, remember that you started your project from nothing, knowing little and understanding even less. You have moved on.

It is not possible to stand still in research, let alone move backwards, so don't have any fear that you might be doing so.

MAKE A NUISANCE OF YOURSELF

Ask for help and advice from your supervisor at every opportunity. It is his or her job to look after you so you might as well make your presence felt and exploit this personal and devoted resource. Your time is short so you have every right to demand attention, provided of course that you are polite, civil, considerate and observing of appointments. Your supervisor will be intensely irritated by lateness, rudeness, sloppy work and indolence but cannot legitimately complain about being confronted by enthusiasm, an inquiring mind or requests for assistance.

STAGE

4

PRESENTING IT

CHAPTER 9

WRITING IT UP

 GETTING STARTED

Writing is a tough and challenging business. Writers of all kinds, with the possible exception of tabloid journalists and some romantic novelists, find the production of convincing and satisfying prose to be an exhausting and emotional activity. This is true not only of 'creative' writers such as novelists, journalists, popular historians and biographers but also of those whose daily toil entails the production of factual material or reports, such as secretaries, legal drafters, scientists, engineers and academics. Writing is joined up thinking and is very, very difficult.

Why is writing so difficult? Words are extraordinarily powerful and like all powerful things, from motorbikes to democracies, they demand skill, energy and concentration if they are to be properly controlled. Words are powerful because they have the ability to transfer ideas from one mind to another over distance and time. In fact, they are the ultimate facilitators of *action at a distance*. To do this reliably and unambiguously they have to be chosen carefully, used precisely and ordered correctly.

The language constructions we use in speech, first assimilated in early childhood and used with minimal thought thereafter, are of only limited value when it comes to committing ideas to paper. Written expression requires different skills. Words on paper have to survive by themselves, out of context, without support from facial expression, body language or the opportunity to ask for further information. Unlike spoken utterances, our written words must survive long beyond the moment of their creation and may even (if we are lucky or unfortunate) outlive us entirely. To make them robust enough to survive requires practice and an unaccustomed energy.

In writing up your dissertation you will need to be both a factual

121

reporter and a creative writer. At the factual end of the scale you need to report the reasons why you did the research, what you did and what results you obtained. At the other extreme, some creativity will be required in presenting your interpretation of the literature, in evaluating your results, and in discussing the wider significance of what your work shows. You will want to ensure that something of yourself is contained in the work.

As your writing proceeds you will develop your own style. This will be coloured by your reading and the style conventions of your subject, by the comments and feedback of your supervisor, and by an on-going increase in your personal awareness of words. You may well find it easiest to start the writing process by taking a factual approach, allowing creativity and personality to develop within your writing as your confidence as a wordsmith progresses.

 HOW LONG WILL IT TAKE?

Earlier on, when discussing time management, it was suggested that you devote one third of your total project time to writing-up. That probably seemed an over-estimate. Now that the writing-up stage is upon you, you may be starting to feel that it was not such an unreasonable proportion after all. Experienced supervisors commonly report that students under-estimate the time needed, not only for writing itself but also for the final production of the dissertation. So the general advice is: **start early**.

You have probably already started your write-up by doing some or all of the following:

☐   Producing interim reports, for your supervisor and/or assessment;
☐   Making notes in your ideas book;
☐   Keeping a project diary;
☐   Maintaining a lab or report book;
☐   Writing up methods and analyses as you did them;
☐   Doing the refocusing exercise (Box 7.2 on page 111)

Don't underestimate the value of these items, even if you feel you want to begin with a clean sheet.

Finally, when trying to work out how long things will take, leave plenty of time for redrafting. You will want to set aside chunks of writing for reconsideration and for the later incorporation of your supervisor's comments.

■ PROCRASTINATION

Without doubt, you will have at your disposal an intimidating battery of personal excuses for deferring the start of your dissertation write-up or for putting off starting on a particular section. These reasons may be:

☐ quasi-rational:
  – 'I've never written anything like this before and don't know where to start';
  – 'I can't get access to the computer room just now'.

☐ diversional:
  – 'I've only got a few minutes before lunch';
  – 'I haven't collected all the data yet'.

☐ perfectionist:
  – 'I'm not very good at writing';
  – 'My supervisor won't like what I've produced'.

☐ irrational:
  – 'I don't know how to type';
  – 'I promised to help my friend mend the car'.

Using, manipulating and justifying these excuses is quite normal. Everyone uses them. They undoubtedly amount to a highly adaptable skill, though probably not one you would wish to be included in the skills list in Chapter 2. Their importance seems to be distorted and accentuated by the inherent difficulty of the writing process, by the fact that you will be assessed on what you write and by the pristine blankness of the screen or page in front of you.

Help is at hand, however. Just as you have the skills of procrastination, you already possess the skills for overcoming them. If you had been unable to overcome these feelings in the past you would not have reached this stage in your academic career. A few minutes spent reflecting on times when you have managed to break the mental logjam should convince you of this. If none of that seems very relevant to your present problems you might try some of the following:

☐ Allow yourself to do something unproductive without feeling guilty about it.
☐ Draft out a brief table of contents; get some highlighting pens and mark the items like traffic lights: *red* for 'Wouldn't touch it with barge pole', *yellow* for 'Might be possible if I got down to it'

and *green* for 'I could make a start here' (see also Box 5.4 on page 60).

☐ Draw a picture of yourself at work on your project; label it with arrows and annotations describing what you are doing.

☐ Go and talk to someone on your hit list (Box 7.1 on page 111): ask them to set you a target or words of pages to be written before you meet them in the bar.

☐ Flick through your ideas book.

☐ Bring your project diary up to date.

☐ Switch off the radio.

☐ Work backwards: write the concluding summary sentence of what you want to say and then build up statements of the evidence you have for it.

☐ Put up a few keywords on the screen, run the Thesaurus over them and see what thoughts are generated in your mind.

☐ Stick a large sheet of paper to the wall, fill it with a graffiti of keywords related to your subject and then draw some lines to make a kind of route map illustrating your progress through the work.

☐ Say what you are trying to say out loud or into a tape-recorder/ Dictaphone; transcribe what you have recorded.

Whatever you do, do something. Make the screen dirty with words. Sully the page. Realize that you are starting, not finishing off, so the quality of what you produce doesn't matter for the moment.

If procrastination remains a stumbling block despite your best endeavours, get help from your supervisor, your tutor or someone else with whom you can discuss your work. If you are feeling uncertain about what you should be doing or whether what you are doing has any value, get a second opinion. You may even find that you have been putting off or worrying about doing something that doesn't need to be done at all.

■ HOW LONG SHOULD IT BE?

Your department may set rules about length. These may relate to the total work or to individual sections. If so, find out right at the start what these are and what tolerance there is. Stick rigidly to the rules: it is crazy to have work ignored, or lose marks, simply by ignoring regulations. Some departments give guidelines rather than strict word or page limits or leave it up to the supervisor to suggest an appropriate number of pages for each section of the dissertation.

Ask for guidance on these matters and make use of the advice you are given.

If you are not sure what a given number of pages (or lines or words) represents in terms of information content, have a look at some recently completed examples in your department. Look at the structure of the work, but also read a few paragraphs and get a feel for the density and efficiency of the writing. But beware! Don't assume that your predecessor got it right – there may be things that you would have done differently. Your writing style will be different, so you need to read between the lines and come to your own conclusion about how much space it will take to say what you have to say.

A general rule for report writing of any kind is to: *Make it as long as necessary but as short as possible*.

At first sight, this statement sounds too vacuous to be helpful. In fact, it is one of the most useful pieces of advice you can take. Think about it: your report needs to be **long enough** to tell the reader what he or she needs to know but **short enough** to ensure that he or she reads it. Thus, it is pointless to include useless information, but equally bad to leave essential material out. Similarly, a report which is too long to read might as well not have been written while one which skimps on important detail will make the reader feel that his or her time was wasted.

WRITING STYLE

The best writing is *imperceptible*. In other words, the reader is allowed to concentrate on what is being said, not on the way in which it is written. Imagine an orchestra: if the players are perfectly in tune with one another, you are unaware of the fact and you concentrate on the music. They may play well, they may play badly, there may even be occasional wrong notes; but *you don't even ask yourself* if they are in tune. It's just the same with writing: any spelling errors, textual irregularities or ungainly phrasing will knock the reader off course and make them conscious of the words rather than the content.

Good writing also carries the reader along whatever their background. This means, on the one hand, that the arguments are clear, logical and explained in easy-to-follow but non-patronizing steps, and, on the other, that few assumptions are made about prior knowledge or accepted dogma. A useful aphorism, often given to new lecturers but equally applicable here, advises that one should: 'Always underestimate the audience's knowledge but never underestimate its intelligence'.

The style you use depends partly on the subject you are writing about and the conventions employed in your discipline area (science, engineering, humanities, arts, etc.). You can get the best advice on this by studying examples from the literature you are working on. Choose some pieces which you have found particularly interesting and exciting and spend a few moments reading between the lines. Consider how the ideas are put together, how the sentence and paragraph structure relates to the presentation of those ideas. Compare these pieces with some that you have written. What levels of explanation are provided? How fast do they carry the reader along? How frequently are adjectives, adverbs and colloquialisms used? Does your own work sound as though it is written by one person? Read it out loud – does it sound as though the reader is meant to understand it?

There are several excellent, unstuffy and readable books on effective writing and good style. Try especially Kirkman (1992), Palmer (1993), Turk and Kirkman (1989), Fairbairn and Winch (1996), Williams (1996). Their advice will help you to improve all types of writing, not just your dissertation. Individual points of style are discussed in a more academic manner in McArthur (1996). Creme and Lea (1997) discuss the characteristics of 'academic' style. Orna and Stevens (1995) provide guidance on organizing and arranging information and on effective page and document design.

FOUR GOALS FOR EFFECTIVE WRITING

Whatever your subject or inherited style, there are four goals to aim at if you want to be an effective writer:

1. Simplicity
Write in such a way that your work can be read by the uninformed as well as the informed reader. This is a difficult task because for the past few months you have been immersing yourself in the subject to a great depth. You now have to step back and explain what it is all about to those who understand it much less deeply. Here are some ways to simplifying your writing style:

❐   Make a mind journey: imagine yourself back to the time before you started work and recall the uninitiated state in which you found yourself. With the possible exception of your supervisor, all your readers will be in that state when they pick up your weighty tome for the first time; you need to make your writing, and therefore your subject, accessible to them.

❐   Practise (and practice!) the arcane but surprisingly useful art of précis. Whenever you write something, think about how you could write it with fewer words. Content is rarely lost by this process and clarity is invariably improved. Far from being a dull school exercise whose sole purpose is a reduction of length, précis can be a highly constructive process: the result should be prose in which every word, every sentence and every paragraph are indispensable to the meaning being conveyed.

❐   Find a friendly and unsuspecting first- or second-year student and ask them to read some of your draft write-up. Later on, a few questions over a glass of something will ascertain whether your style is understandable.

❐   Do the refocusing exercise (Box 7.2 on page 111).

2. Clarity
Aim to get your message across clearly and make it as readable as possible. This means:

❐   Using chapters with a well-defined structure, breaking the chapter up into manageable sub-sections with sub-headings to guide the reader and building paragraphs around a single idea or argument.

❐   Using short sentences and words which are easy to understand (explaining complex ideas does not mean that you have to use complex sentences!).

❐   Setting the scene effectively by giving clear aims, objectives and hypotheses.

❐   Avoiding clichés and jargon.

❐   Explaining all abbreviations and acronyms.

❐   Being economical with words; use the simplest word you can find compatible with the idea you are trying to express; remove unnecessary words, especially qualifiers and tautologies.

❐   Removing over-frequent or unwanted reference citations, quotations, footnotes, etc.

3. Accuracy
Present the facts, or the current view of the facts, as honestly as you can and give your reader all the information he or she needs to know. This advice sounds almost too commonplace to be worth stating ('the truth, the whole truth, and nothing but the truth'), but it is worth thinking about. It really means distinguishing between what is known and what is your own or someone else's speculation.

Make your arguments convincing by backing them up with balanced evidence. A good rule to follow is that **every** statement you make (that is, every sentence you write) should be **externally justified** in one or more of the following ways:

- ❑ by reference to a published source;
- ❑ by easily followed logic from a previous statement;
- ❑ by evidence you have obtained yourself.

(There is one exception to this: statements of such commonplace knowledge that a reference would, within the context, insult the reader; for example, 'Words are made of letters', 'Cows have four legs', 'Shakespeare wrote plays'.)

If what you want to say cannot be justified in one of these ways, it is speculation and must be clearly identified as such. By following this advice you will avoid any danger of plagiarism (see p. 145 later in this chapter).

4. Precision

Provide good quality information, get straight to the point and don't be vague. Make it clear to the reader how confident you are about the statements you make. Indicate the appropriate level of confidence by:

- ❑ retaining detail;
- ❑ avoiding exaggeration;
- ❑ pointing out important distinctions and differences;
- ❑ avoiding unwarranted generalizations;
- ❑ saying what you mean;
- ❑ avoiding colloquialisms, similes and metaphors (except to illustrate a specific idea).

Remember:

- ❑ Information which is vague or understated is useless.
- ❑ Information which is too detailed or overstated is useless.

With **numerical data**, precision is expressed by:

- ❑ using an appropriate number of decimal places (*remember*: giving too many is untruthful, while giving too few is obfuscatory; either fault misleads the reader);
- ❑ stating confidence limits;
- ❑ using a statistical test to distinguish significant events from chance variation.

So remember also:

- ❑ Numerical data which lacks statistical backup is useless.

Box 9.1 explains the difference between accuracy and precision.

Box 9.1   Accuracy and precision

Definitions: Accuracy – Nearness to the truth
Precision – Confident and appropriate expression of detail

Your work should be both accurate and precise, but the two qualities are unrelated. To avoid misleading the reader, take care of them separately.

Example 1: Dog bites man
What really happened:

> The postman walked up the drive at breakfast time with several letters in his hand ready for delivery. The door of the house opened unexpectedly and an Alsatian ran out. The Alsatian bit the postman on the right calf and ran off down the street. The postman needed five stitches and was off work for a fortnight.

Accurate but imprecise report:

> A man was attacked by an animal in the course of his work. He was seriously injured and did not appear for several days.

Precise but inaccurate report:

> The postman arrived at 11.57 AM to deliver three parcels wrapped in brown paper. A small, brown dog jumped out of the open living room window and bit the milkman, leaving a neat row of teeth marks in the side of his left hand. The dog was called inside by its owner, a woman in a blue dressing gown, who then attended to the injured milkman and shocked postman. Neither man was able to work for 15.5 days.

Example 2: Election result
What really happened:

> Result after four recounts:
> Labour candidate   20 567 votes
> Conservative candidate   20 566 votes
> Liberal Democrat candidate 11 243 votes

Accurate but imprecise headline:

> Lib-Dems lose after several recounts

Precise but inaccurate headline:

> Labour undisputed winners with 29.2679853% of vote
> (get a calculator . . .)

DRAFTING AND REDRAFTING

It will take you several attempts to get your writing as you want it. Simplicity, clarity, accuracy and precision are never optimally achieved the first time something is written. This is because both your writing skill and your ideas develop as you go along. Writing one section affects the content of others, and you may not fully understand the point you are making until you have tried to put it into words in several different ways. As a result, you should *expect* to redraft your work a number of times.

You can rake through your writing as you go, say after each paragraph, stripping out redundancies and choosing more appropriate words (think of your prose as a grass lawn infested with moss). This is a wise approach, but there will come a point when you can no longer see what you are doing. When this happens, mark the section of text with some >>>chevrons<<< (or a highlighting pen or a Post-it note if it is printed out), put it away for a day or two and go on to another section. When you come back to it, see if it still says what you want it to say and see if it still has the correct context within the rest of the material. Particularly recalcitrant pieces may have to be revisited in this way several times over. You will also want to incorporate your supervisor's comments. The word-processor makes all this very easy to handle, even fun.

DESCRIBING YOUR METHODS: VOICE AND CONTENT

Writing up the methods section of your dissertation can cause some particular difficulties. For one thing, the style you need to adopt may be quite different (drier, more factual) from that which is appropriate elsewhere. You may also be uncertain about the level of detail which you need to put in. Your supervisor can advise you about specific styles appropriate to your subject and you can look at previous dissertations in your department for examples of what is needed.

In general, the following rules are safe to follow (see Table 9.1):

❑ Provide sufficient detail that someone else could do what you have done and reasonably expect to get the same result.

❑ Consign tedious, repetitive detail to tables (perhaps in an appendix).

❒   Leave out extraneous details.
❒   Leave out results (these go in the results section).
❒   Leave out reasoning (this goes in the introduction and discussion sections).
❒   Use the **impersonal, passive** voice and keep to the past tense.

Following these rules does not make for particularly attractive writing, but that is not your aim at this point. And if tables and diagrams are more appropriate than words then use them. The purpose of this section is to record what you did as clearly, fully and unambiguously as possible. It is a reference section: your readers will consult it for factual information, not for entertainment or cultural gratification.

Table 9.1 Examples of appropriate and inappropriate styles for describing methods	
Appropriate style	*Inappropriate style*
'The subject breathed forcibly into a Haldane tube and a sample of expired air was obtained using a gas-proof syringe (Impermeable Plastics Ltd, Dagenham) from a three-way tap (Brilliant Fittings Ltd, Penge) attached to the proximal end of the tube. The CO_2 concentration (volume %) in the sample was measured using an infra-red gas analyser (Model A123, Hobson Instruments, Bradford).'	'I asked Philippa, my lab partner, to breathe forcibly into the blue-grey coloured Haldane tube so that I could take a sample of her expired air from the end of the tube nearest her mouth. The CO_2 content of expired air is measured using an infra-red gas analyser. It was about 3.2%. This is a higher value than that reported for marathon runners by Watson and Crich (1986) and showed that Philippa is not as fit as she thinks she is.'

For practical methods involving equipment, chemicals or other materials obtained from outside, it is good practice to give full details of specifications and suppliers. This may include a catalogue number and will usually include a company name and town. (If the same supplier is referred to more than once, just state the town the first time.) Gathering these details can be tedious and surprisingly time-consuming but it needs to be done. Once again, the reason for doing this is to enable others to repeat your work if they wish. You may feel that your results could have been obtained with any one of a dozen similar instruments, but you have no direct evidence for this so be cautious. It would be embarrassing to make a measurement of some important parameter and then find that the instrument you used had been incorrectly calibrated by the manufacturer. Shift the responsibility to their (broader) shoulders by giving full details of the instrument type and where it came from.

 ## THE MECHANICS OF WRITING

Another golden rule:

> The only sensible way to write up your dissertation is by drafting it directly to the computer.

If this frightens you, or you feel that you might be too slow or inefficient, note the following:

- ❐ You need to know how to word-process, but you are not trying to learn how to type. If you can already type, all well and good. If you can't, you will soon learn albeit using only a few fingers. This is the way the majority of us work, so you are in good company. At the writing stage, it is rare for thoughts to float by so quickly that even a slow, two-finger typist could not catch them.

- ❐ Don't just use the word-processor to produce a final copy. Think of it as a creative tool. Use it to organize your thoughts and to give you a visual impression of how things are shaping up as you go along. Word-processors allow you to experiment with your writing, to try different words, different arrangements of words and different formats.

- ❐ Use paper to scribble down notes and rough diagrams but reach for the keyboard as soon as complete sentences start to form.

- ❐ Look upon word-processing as a skill-development exercise: people who can't use a word-processor seldom make it to the job shortlist; people who can't type frequently do.

The advantage provided by the word-processor's efficiency in manipulating text *far exceeds* any short-term disadvantage in needing to learn how to use it. It allows you to spend less time drafting and re-drafting and more time thinking about what you really want to say. As mentioned before, few of us can type properly, but that doesn't seem to matter – our keyboard fluency and productivity have increased nonetheless. This means, as far as your project write-up is concerned, that you have to equip **yourself** with the skills and knowledge needed to produce something attractive, readable and free of errors. And on the other side of the same coin, the high specification of modern word-processors and printers means that there is really **no excuse** for producing work which is of anything less than true professional quality.

SCALING UP THE PRODUCTION

In all likelihood, you have already been producing coursework in word-processed format and you may indeed feel confident in the minutiae of desk-top publication. What you may find, however, is that the size of the work you now have to create takes you into new or unfamiliar areas of text production. For example, you will have to maintain a consistency of style (headings, section numbering, diagram indexing, citation referencing, etc.) for the duration of a large-scale document; this needs forethought and awareness. The simple fact of needing to work at the keyboard for long periods may itself put new demands on your powers of concentration.

There is no doubt at all that your keyboard skills will grow substantially as you proceed, even if at first progress seems slow. Box 9.2 provides a checklist of word-processing features that you will find useful. In bringing your word-processing skills up to speed your aim should be to control and exploit the technology, not to be limited or frustrated by it.

You can help yourself in fairly obvious ways, for example by:

❏ keeping with one machine and one type of software as far as possible;

❏ making sure from the outset that your printer connection is reliable;

❏ making regular *but judicious* use of spelling and grammar checkers;

❏ dividing your work up into several files (chapters, experiments, or whatever comes naturally) rather than trying to work on the whole document at once;

and of course by:

❏ making frequent saves and regular back-ups.

Box 9.2   Basic word-processing features

This is a list of the minimum features you will need on your word-processor. Check that you know how to use them without consulting the manual or the Help menu.

Where possible, set the button bar to give you direct access to each feature.

☐   Layout

Font type and size
Line spacing
Page layout and margins
Superscripts, subscripts, special characters
Paragraph indents
Bullets and numbers
Page numbering

☐   View

Page width
Full page/print preview

☐   Writing tools

Cut, copy and paste
Search (Find) and replace
Spell checker
Grammar checker
Thesaurus

☐   Objects

Tables
Text boxes
Diagrams
Linking and embedding objects

☐   Document tools

Create table of contents
Create index
Automatic timed back-up

☐   Document information

Word count
Page count

Most importantly, you should be clear about the format you are aiming for **right from the start**. As with experimental design, a little anticipation in this area can help you to avoid annoying mistakes and the irritation of wasting time over unnecessary textual revision. You want to put your energies into saying what you have to say and redrafting it for maximum effect, not into continually revising the structure or appearance of the document.

USING SPELLING AND GRAMMAR CHECKERS

These word-processing tools always look as if they can banish your literacy problems for ever, but unfortunately they can't. They can certainly be helpful, but only when used wisely. They are a bit like electronic calculators for arithmetic – unless you know the sort of answer you are expecting, you can be easily misled.

The spelling checker will always detect:

☐ typos and mis-spellings which do not, by chance, mean something else;
☐ words which do not appear in the software manufacturer's vocabulary;
☐ inadvertent duplication ('Shall I compare thee to a a summer's day?');

but will not spot:

☐ words used in the wrong context ('Shall I compare thee with a summer's day?');
☐ errors which happen to be real words (their/there, meat/meet, plural/pleural, effect/affect);
☐ inconsistently used alternatives (ionised/ionized, physiologic/ physiological);
☐ nouns which should be adjectives (dependant/dependent, mucus/ mucous);
☐ incorrect expressions which have become locally or colloquially acceptable (orient/orientate, alternate/alternative);

and will probably infuriate you by picking up:

☐ words which are spelled differently in different cultures (colour/ color, tyre/tire);
☐ usual names, especially in citations and references;
☐ specialist abbreviations;

however careful you have been in specifying its menu settings.

Grammar checkers are even more difficult to exploit. They usually work to strict academic rules but may allow the user to set the 'level' of scrutiny or the professional context (legal, scientific, etc.). They present three main problems:

- ❏ They have a built-in notion of what a good sentence looks like (length, use of commas, number of subordinate clauses, etc.) which may not conform to your own.
- ❏ They work on the literal meanings of words and may not accommodate colloquial usage.
- ❏ The explanation of your apparent error may be difficult to understand (what *is* a subordinate clause?) without a degree in linguistics.

Many of the faults which the grammar checker throws up may be significant, and avoiding these will improve your prose, but distinguishing the useful from the fatuous may take more effort than you expect. It would often be better to spend time checking your grammar in other ways such as by reading out loud or getting a friend to look at it. Note also that grammar and spelling checkers, especially the sort which correct as you type, can significantly retard word-processors running on computers with older chips and limited memory.

In the end, spelling and grammar checkers can diagnose and suggest but cannot treat – you as writer remain responsible for what is written. Use these tools for reference and as traps for gremlins, but accept their ~~advise~~ advice and ~~assistante~~ assistance judiciously.

WHAT FORMAT SHOULD I USE?

You need to be concerned with the following aspects of format:

- ❏ Length
- ❏ Arrangement of sections and numbering
- ❏ Font, font size, line spacing, margins and page numbering
- ❏ Presentation of data and diagrams
- ❏ Labelling of illustrations and legend details
- ❏ Presentation of the abstract
- ❏ Use and content of appendices
- ❏ Use of footnotes
- ❏ Citation systems
- ❏ Tables of contents and indices
- ❏ Title page details
- ❏ Method of binding

Your department or faculty may have strict rules about many or all of these things. If so, make sure you know what they are and abide by them. Some of them (for example, use or avoidance of footnotes, citation systems, legend details) may be determined by convention within your own subject area and there may be specific rules of citation which you need to follow. Again you need to find out what is acceptable right from the outset, probably by talking to your supervisor or by looking at (reliable) examples of earlier dissertations.

If no regulations are set, Box 9.3 suggests a commonly acceptable dissertation/thesis format. It is built around sections similar to those you would find in a research paper, particularly in the pure and applied sciences. Even if the overall format of the dissertation is negotiable, the division of material among the sections must be strictly adhered to: as with a research paper, the reader needs to know precisely where to find specific types of information.

REFERENCE CITATION

Box 9.4 explains some commonly used systems of reference citation applicable in the sciences. Others can be found in Fowler *et al.* (1998). Note that you usually have a choice between name and number systems but be sure that you use only one and use it consistently. There are advantages and disadvantages associated with each, as indicated in Table 9.2. Most authors find the flexibility of the Harvard system to be a crucial factor in the decision.

When constructing the bibliography, you will need to decide on a level of punctuation and abbreviation. Box 9.5 suggests and illustrates some common ones. They are all acceptable, subject as usual to local guidelines or rules, but decide on one and be consistent. If you chose to abbreviate journal names, use a recognized system. The principles of abbreviation are given by British Standard 4148 (ask in the library). Lists of abbreviated journal names can be found in several of the bibliographical guide books held by your library such as:

❑ *Serial Sources for the BIOSIS Previews Database*, BIOSIS, Philadelphia.
❑ *World List of Scientific Periodicals*, Butterworths, London.
❑ *Serials in the British Library*.
❑ *Science Citation Index, Social Sciences Citation Index* and *Arts & Humanities*.
❑ *Citation Index*, ISI, Philadelphia.

Box 9.3   A commonly acceptable thesis/dissertation format

Textual style

Paper:	A4, white, portrait orientation, one side only
Text:	Times New Roman, 11 or 12 point
Spacing:	Line spacing 1.5 or 2
Margins:	Left and right 2.5 cm; top and bottom 2.5 cm
Page numbers:	Bottom right corner, suppressed on title page.

Either   Arabic throughout,

or   Lower case Roman for Abstract, Acknowledgements, Contents pages, etc; Arabic for main text and all subsequent pages

Section numbering: Arabic numbers, levels indicated by decimal separation,

e.g.   1.1
      1.1.1
      1.1.2
      1.2
      2.1, etc.

Order and content of sections

Title page: Title, author's full name, departmental address, institution, date.
May need an institutional statement: 'Dissertation completed in partial fulfilment of the requirements for . . .'

Abstract/Summary: Less than one side of text. Must come immediately after Title page.
Must be self-sustaining – no incomplete citations or unexplained abbreviations (*best*: no citations or abbreviations at all).

Acknowledgements: The only personal part of the work.
Be brief, complete, polite, professional and avoid obscure witticisms.

Table of Contents: After Acknowledgements, preceding main text.
Devolve to major sub-headings. Indent each sub-section level.
Separate tables of illustrations, data tables, appendices.

Abbreviations: Optional; on a separate page preceding the main text. An alphabetical list using commonly accepted abbreviations where possible.

Main text: Introduction, literature, aims, methods, results, discussion, conclusions.

References: All works cited in the text. Nothing else.

Box 9.3 Continued	
Appendices:	For collections of raw data, methodological details, statistical and mathematical calculations, etc., referred to in main text. Numbered or lettered (upper case) sequentially.

Illustrations (Figures and Tables)

Numbering:	*Either* Figure 1 ... n, Table 1 ... n
	or Figure N.1 ... N.n, Table N.1 ... Nn, where N is the chapter number.
Labelling:	A short piece of descriptive text. Can use smaller font size (8 or 9)
	Must make content of illustration understandable without reference to main text.

REFERENCING WWW AND INTERNET SITES

Using World Wide Web pages and internet sites (newsgroups, discussion groups, etc.) as sources of information for research requires special care. Recognize first and foremost that such sites are un-refereed and that the information they contain is very unlikely to have been subjected to any kind of expert scrutiny or peer review. Even the information published by 'moderated' sites has usually only been checked for acceptability, not veracity. This makes such sources intrinsically **unreliable** compared with other published material. Secondly, be aware that WWW sites are inherently **unstable**. The owner of the site can, and probably will, update or modify its content on a regular basis (the immediacy and transience of the medium are two of its great attractions). A site's location can change at any time and may even be shut down altogether. Unlike conventional library or archive material, it may not be there next time you or your reader needs it.

Bearing these caveats in mind, although the WWW and the Internet may be valuable resources, it would be unwise to base key aspects of your research on the information they hold. If you do need to cite a WWW page for example, be sure to give in your bibliography:

❐ the full address, usually starting with *http://* and giving the **complete** names of **all** sub-pages (*NB:* some web browsers routinely truncate page addresses on the screen, especially if they have more than a very small number of 'slash' (/) dividers);

❐ any source date attached to the article;

❐ the full date (day/month/year) on which you last accessed the location;

Box 9.4   Literature citation systems

Choose one of the following, referring to Table 9.2 for the advantages and disadvantages of each.

Either the name ('Harvard') system:

'Smith (1996) showed that . . .'
'It has been shown (Smith, 1996) that . . .'
'. . . as several authors have shown (Grey, 1992; White and Brown, 1994)'
Citation for work with more than two authors:

> *First time*   'Smith, Jones and Wilson (1994)';
> *thereafter*   'Smith *et al.* (1994)'.

Use an alphabetical bibliography.

Or the number system:

'Smith (25) showed that . . .'
'It has been shown (25) that . . .'
'. . . as several authors have shown (15, 34)'.
Numbering: *either*   in order of appearance in text
                     (place in number order in bibliography)
             or   in order of appearance in alphabetical
                     bibliography.
Numbers can be as superscripts if preferred provided that no other superscripts (arithmetic powers, footnote markers, etc.) will be encountered.
Use a numerical bibliography.

Rules for alphabetical bibliography

Alphabetical by first author name, *then*:
Single author before joint authors, date order (a, b, c, etc. for more than one in a single year).
Two authors before more than two, date order.

Rules for a numerical bibliography

Either: Numbered in the order of first appearance in the text.
Or: Numbered in alphabetical order.

Bibliography style and details

As in the Bibliography for this book.
See also Box 9.5.

Table 9.2   Advantages and disadvantages of the name and number systems of citation

System	Advantages	Disadvantages
Citation by name (the Harvard system)	Presence of the authors' names in text continually refreshes the memory as you read.	Takes up significant space in the text.
	Inserting/deleting citations has no effect on order of references in the bibliography.*	May look repetitive and can interrupt flow, especially when many citations comes together.
Citation by number	Takes little space.	Number give no immediate information on author or date.
	Less distracting to the reader.	Can be confused with other text notation (ranges in parentheses, arithmetical symbols, etc.).
		Minor changes to citation in text will occasion a drastic reordering/ renumbering of references.*

*In practice, this criterion may make you decide in favour of citation by name.

- ☐ the title of the page or article;
- ☐ the name and professional affiliation of any individual associated with the article;
- ☐ the name of the organization hosting the site (this may not be obvious from the site address).

As with all other referencing operations, your aims are (a) to absolve yourself from any direct responsibility for the material and (b) to provide sufficient information for someone else to locate it.

Box 9.5   Levels of punctuation and abbreviation in citations

Choose one of the following styles, or one which gives an equivalent amount of information, and stick to it. Some of the differences are very subtle.

If you decide to abbreviate journal names, make sure (a) that your abbreviations conform to British Standard 4148 or some other accepted list, (b) that you always abbreviate, and (c) that you always use the same abbreviation. To avoid ambiguity, always include the punctuation in abbreviated journal names.

Winton, D., Monkhouse, R., Meg, M. & Wogan, T. (1997), A comparison of visually alluring procedures for extending the televisual delivery of superficial or intrinsically limited data. *Journal of Stochastic Data Presentation*, **8** (5), 10–20.

Winton, D., Monkhouse, R., Meg, M. & Wogan, T. (1997) A comparison of visually alluring procedures for extending the televisual delivery of superficial or intrinsically limited data. *J. Stoch. Data Pres.*, **8** (5), 10–20.

Winton D., Monkhouse R., Meg M. and Wogan T. (1997) A comparison of visually alluring procedures for extending the televisual delivery of superficial or intrinsically limited data. *Journal of Stochastic Data Presentation*, **8** (5) 10–20.

Winton D, Monkhouse R, Meg M & Wogan T (1997) A comparison of visually alluring procedures for extending the televisual delivery of superficial or intrinsically limited data *Journal of Stochastic Data Presentation* **8** (5) 10–20.

Winton D, Monkhouse R, Meg M & Wogan T (1997) A comparison of visually alluring procedures for extending the televisual delivery of superficial or intrinsically limited data *J. Stoch. Data Pres.* **8** (5) 10–20

FANCY FORMATTING

Word-processors and bibliographic databases, as suggested earlier, make many aspects of the formatting process easy to set and adjust. They can even take the slog out of creating tables of contents and indices. If you are really skilled, you can do fancy things like embedding diagrams, scanning in pictures (but beware copyright!) and adding running page headers. These kinds of embellishments, provided they fall within departmental regulations, can make your final report look really professional and outstanding. Be sure, however, that you know what you are doing before you commit yourself to the extra time and expense involved – you can quickly reach the point where a law of diminishing returns takes hold. Even more importantly, be sure that the *underlying* material is sound: a dissertation which is beset by spelling errors, unattributed citations or poor paragraph layout will not be rescued by colour pictures and a sexy typeface.

PRESENTING DATA: ILLUSTRATIONS

Your dissertation will essentially be a production in text, but illustrations will find an important place. Some of the information you want to present to the reader will naturally take a visual form. This applies most obviously to the results section but to other parts of the dissertation as well. For example, there may be chunks of the literature which can be summarized in a table more effectively than as a block of heavily referenced text. Similarly, routine analytical methods and their associated quality control data can often be more accessible in tabular or diagrammatic form.

Pages of unbroken text can be hard going for the reader, however eloquent the writing. On the other hand, illustrations need to be used effectively and in such a way that the reader is encouraged to look at them. A run of pages with charts and diagrams, inserted *en bloc* in the middle of otherwise continuous text, can be disconcerting; distributing them with care among the particular parts of the text to which they refer is much more inviting. At every stage of putting your write-up together, think about which method of presenting information is going to be the most effective.

Some general rules for illustrations:

❏   Every illustration must be referred to in the text (otherwise it will not be looked at and might as well not be there!).

❏   Present information *either* in words *or* as an illustration (table, chart, diagram, photograph, etc.), but not both. The text referring to the illustration may contain a brief summary of what is shown, but it should not duplicate the information.

❏   Every illustration must have a legend (caption).

❏   Illustrations must be able to stand alone. The legend must contain a clear, concise statement of what is shown and must fully explain any abbreviations or symbols. It should not, on the other hand, contain any interpretation of the data. As a guide, someone with no prior knowledge of the subject who opens the dissertation at a particular illustration should be able to understand its content, but not necessarily its meaning, without reference to the text.

☐ For pictures and photos, be sure to include any essential scale references and acknowledge the sources of copied material.

☐ One illustration per page is usually enough and there should certainly be no more than two.

☐ Only have text and illustration on the same page if you can do it neatly, spaciously and without compromising the size of the illustration or its legend. It is also unwise to end up with less than three lines of text on the page. If in doubt, give the illustration its own page. (Take note of local regulations: these sometimes specify separate pages for illustrations.)

☐ Put the legend immediately above (tables) or below (other illustrations) the illustration. Use a slightly smaller typeface and indent both ends of the line to bring it to the width of the illustration.

☐ Make each illustration easy to understand by (a) minimizing the amount of information, (b) keeping the order and orientation of the information logical, intuitive and consistent.

☐ Use a consistent set of symbols and abbreviations for variables which appear in more than one illustration. (Make sure that all abbreviations have been clearly defined.)

☐ Use colour only (a) if it is needed to distinguish different elements of the data, (b) if your printer can do it easily, clearly and consistently. If you find yourself needing to use too many colours, types of symbol or styles of shading (say, more than three) in a single chart or diagram, it is a sign that you are trying to include too much information. Remember also that colour rarely photocopies well.

☐ Pictorial representations of numerical data (graphs, histograms, pie charts, etc.) require special thought. There may be several possible ways of orientating and displaying the data, but the simplest is always the best.

☐ With quantified experimental data, distinguish between dependent and independent variables and assign them correctly to the ordinate and abscissa.

☐ Label all axes. Use the minimum number of tick marks compatible with understanding the scale. Indicate broken or truncated scales adequately.

❏ For data points based on a mean, always provide an estimate of variability, state how it was obtained (the statistical test used) and give the number of replicates.

❏ When graphing continuous variables, be sure to state how any interpolations or lines of best fit were derived (for example, least squares, non-linear regression, by hand, etc.).

❏ Data in tables can be arranged vertically or horizontally with respect to the dependent and independent variables, but be consistent. If you have a choice it is usually better to have fewer columns and more rows than vice versa. For best visual effect, separate column headings from data by a horizontal line but keep other lines, especially vertical ones, to a minimum.

PLAGIARISM AND FABRICATION

What are they?

Plagiarism is: *The use of someone else's work or material and passing it off as one's own without permission or acknowledgement* or: *Quotation without citation.*

Fabrication is: *Deliberately falsifying data or results* or *Inventing information.*

In other words, **cheating**.

These are very serious academic offences, usually afforded their own clause or chapter in the university rule book. They can be committed at any level of academic activity from entrance exam to doctoral dissertation or beyond. Sociological studies of students, based on frank and anonymous interviews, show that cheating of one kind or another is surprisingly common (Newstead, 1998). The frequency with which it is actually detected is impossible to determine. Accusations are rare, probably because the demands of proof are difficult to sustain but also because most people like a quiet life. But they do occur. And any academic will tell you that he or she is regularly presented with coursework which appears to be of doubtful parentage.

Plagiarism and fabrication are not unknown even among professional researchers, as a number of high-profile cases over the years have testified. Perhaps the worst examples would be the deliberate copying of someone else's research data to achieve professional advancement or the invention of misleading safety data by a drug company for the purposes of product licensing. Needless to say, it is not the aim of this section to warn you about extreme practices such as these.

As far as student work is concerned the main problem is that plagiarism and fabrication can be committed at a range of levels and with varying degrees of intent. For convenience, we can divide these into deliberate and inadvertent (Table 9.3), but they really form a continuum. The indiscretions listed as 'inadvertent' become 'deliberate' the moment you become aware of them.

Table 9.3 Examples of plagiarism and fabrication applicable to student work	
Deliberate	*Inadvertent*
Copying all or part of another student's work.	Including the results of a joint effort without explanation.
Passing off one student's work as another's.	
Unacknowledged reproduction of all or part of a published work.	Using verbatim unattributed passages from papers or books.
Quotation without citation.	Forgetting to include a reference, or giving incorrect or incomplete details of the source.
Citing a source you have not read or seen yourself.	Attributing a source not to its originator but to a later author or reviewer.
Reproducing an illustration without permission.	Listing a reference which has no citation.
Using downloaded Internet material without reference to source.	Failing to acknowledge a personal communication
Breaching copyright or patent.	Copying tables or diagrams without acknowledgement.
Inventing data, altering existing data or hiding relevant data.	Using an instrument or device invented by someone else without proper attribution.
Deliberately using an inappropriate statistical test or analytical procedure.	Forgetting to cite an original method description.
Massaging data so that it fits a preconception or obscures errors.	Failing to acknowledge technical assistance or other outside help.

Why are they so serious?
Simply because they breach the principles of trust, integrity and commitment to excellence in scholarship upon which academic life is founded. Your degree certificate attests to those principles in the most public manner possible and there is *no other way* of retaining academic rigour.

How can they be avoided?
Avoiding deliberate plagiarism and fabrication is a matter of conscience. Avoiding inadvertent forms depends on awareness, careful record-keeping and attention to detail. Although it will cause you to lose valuable marks during assessment, no one is going to prosecute you or haul you before the vice-chancellor simply for forgetting to reference a citation or acknowledge the source of a diagram. Nevertheless, it is worth remembering that:

☐   deliberate and inadvertent plagiarism/fabrication carry equal responsibility;
☐   detected and undetected plagiarism/fabrication are equally unprofessional;
☐   a dissertation littered with mistakes and omissions loses credibility (as well as marks).

How can they be detected?
Unskilled plagiarism is easy to spot. Well-known passages of text copied verbatim or textbook diagrams will be flagged up by your supervisor without hesitation as soon as they are presented for checking. Your supervisor's eyebrows will also be raised if there is a sudden change (usually for the better!) in writing style or if the quality of otherwise indifferent work suddenly improves.

Skilled (and therefore deliberate) cheating is by definition much more difficult to detect. On the other hand, it is by the same token much more difficult to *produce*. You would really have to put in much quality time and effort, not to mention literary skill, to make someone else's work look and sound like your own. Few worthwhile sources are so obscure that both your supervisor and the examiners of your dissertation are likely never to have read them. Similarly, inventing convincing data and making it internally consistent is extremely difficult (think of all the raw data sheets, the statistical analysis, the need for a realistic level of error...). In all these cases, you might sensibly consider integrity to be the easier option.

In addition to the moderation of your work carried out by your supervisor, there is one important formal occasion when plagiarism may well be detected. That occasion is coming soon and it is the time when you least want to be embarrassed. Your dissertation will be looked at, and very possibly marked, by an external examiner. He or she will probably interview you at some stage and if there is something amiss with your work you can be sure that questions will be asked. You may know that at doctorate level the student's interview with the examiners is often referred to as the 'defence' of the thesis. That's a useful description of what you may be asked to do (although not at such great length). It therefore behoves you to pay great attention to detail in what you write, to understand what you are writing and to make certain that all the statements you make can be justified (see 'Four goals for effective writing – accuracy' earlier in this chapter on page 126).

❐   *Plagiarism?* – Just don't.
❐   *Fabrication?* – Don't even think it.

■ THE ABSTRACT AND SUMMARY: CLOSING THE LOOP

The **Summary** (or 'Conclusions') and the **Abstract** should be the last two parts of the dissertation which you complete. In many ways they are the most difficult to write, but at the same time they are among the most important to get right. They are often the only parts which a casual reader might look at. Even an interested reader might read them in preference to wading through the details in the rest of the work. They are your opportunity to draw attention to what you have done and to encourage the reader to venture further in. You need to set aside adequate time to think about what you want to say and to write them effectively.

The summary comes after the discussion and is a simple way of closing the loop on the whole dissertation. You will not be able to write it until you have identified and dealt with all the matters that need working through in the discussion, so don't try. When you do come to write it, however, you may find that it offers the first opportunity for a complete reflection on what your research project has all been about and the overall progress you have made. In this respect, the summary can be something to look forward to as well as a literary challenge – you can expect to learn some profound things during the process of completing it.

In the summary you should set out to:

❐   answer, or draw conclusions about, all those questions you raised in the list of aims at the start of the work;
❐   provide a summary of any other important observations or conclusions you have made.

Point out the clear answers but don't be afraid to say if questions remain unanswered – these provide valuable material for the next researcher in the subject, just as you used earlier dissertations to get ideas for your work.

The length of the summary is not too important although, as with the rest of your dissertation, brevity is a virtue. The characteristics of a good summary are simplicity, logic and ease of understanding. The best way to achieve this is with bullet points (or a number sequence, if you want to indicate a progression of ideas). Restrict each point to one, or at most two sentences. Where possible, make clear, concise statements and try to avoid repeating the complex arguments and analyses of the discussion.

The abstract will appear immediately after the title page of your dissertation and it therefore has particular prominence. It has to be a summary of the *whole* work, including the reasons for carrying out the study, the methods used, the results obtained and the conclusions arrived at. It really acts as an advertisement. So the abstract is a major exercise in the art of précis, and writing it will prove to be the utmost test of your skill with words.

Length *is* an important consideration in writing the abstract. For a short dissertation, a single paragraph of less than half a side is ideal. For longer works, especially one where there is significant methodological development, aim to keep it to between one half and three quarters of a side of paper. Only under very exceptional circumstances should the abstract extend to a full side or beyond. Aside from matters of style and readability, there is a good practical reason for keeping it short: abstracts are sometimes extracted for on-line presentation by literature search organizations and may be abruptly truncated if too long. Also, readers frequently photocopy abstracts as an easily filed record of the contents of the work; this is obviously a less attractive proposition if it is lengthy.

Keeping your abstract short as you write it can be frustrating: stripping out great swathes of reasoning and experimental detail goes against the grain and you may end up feeling that the result is emaciated and does not properly represent the work from which it came. But you have no choice. The abstract is a summary the sole purpose of which is to indicate **scope** and **content**. Its purpose is not to repeat complex detail or to rehearse long, involved arguments. If readers wish to know these things, they can read the appropriate parts of the dissertation. They will certainly not do so if the abstract itself is over-ambitious or presented in an inaccessible style.

Guidelines for writing a successful abstract:

❐   Aim to write a stand-alone document. It will probably be read that way.

❏ Assume that the reader is very intelligent but knows nothing at all about the subject of your project.

❏ Keep to one paragraph if your abstract is less than half a page. If it is longer, you can use a sequence of paragraphs as a means of organizing what you want to say. In both cases, the paragraphs must be readable and short.

❏ Present information in the same sequence as it appears in the dissertation: introduction, hypothesis, methods, observations and conclusions.

❏ In the case of experimental projects, only include numerical detail if you have obtained absolute values which are of interest beyond the context of *your* experiments.

❏ Avoid tables and diagrams.

❏ Do not expect the reader to make comparisons (for example, between the treatment and control results) or inferences. Make these things explicit and unambiguous.

❏ Use the past tense throughout.

❏ Do not use *any* jargon or unexplained abbreviations.

❏ Avoid literature citations unless absolutely necessary. If a citation is unavoidable, a complete reference must also be given (remember, the abstract will be seen alone).

❏ Start the last sentence or the last paragraph with the words 'In summary, this investigation has shown that' or 'In conclusion, this study has demonstrated that' or something similar.

ERROR CHECKING

Now that your dissertation is written, it is time to check it for errors. Errors will be of two kinds:

1. errors of content (have you written what you meant to write? Are all statements justified and referenced?);
2. errors of presentation (typographical, spelling and formatting errors);

and you need to be on the look out for both.

It will take several attempts to find all your mistakes, and even then you will probably miss some (there is no such thing as a completely error-free document), so set aside some time to do this properly. Assuming that you have made appropriate use of spelling and grammar checkers during the writing process (see 'Using spelling and grammar checkers' earlier in this chapter on page 135), your task now is to find things that the machine would not find. Before you start, you might want to skim once more through some of the books on style and presentation listed in the Bibliography, just to remind yourself what good text looks like.

To detect errors, you will have to try to stand back from the dissertation and read it as if you were new both to the work and to the subject. This turns out to be unexpectedly difficult, and it may be necessary to read it in quite small chunks with long breaks or diversions in between. As soon as the reading becomes *automatic* you are likely to start making sub-conscious assumptions and compensations. If this happens, you will miss things that you would otherwise have spotted.

Try the following techniques for error checking:

- ❐ Place an opaque ruler under each line as you read it so that you obscure your view of what is coming next.
- ❐ Ask someone else to read it; maybe you could swap dissertations with a friend.
- ❐ Read the text backwards, starting at the final full stop. (This technique is obviously restricted to finding presentational errors!)
- ❐ Find somewhere private and read the dissertation out loud to yourself.

THE FINAL DRAFT: WHAT TO LOOK FOR

After the final error check, but some time before the final hand-in date, you need to print out a final draft copy of your complete work for checking. This must be the *complete* work, including title and prefatory pages, all illustrations, the bibliography and appendices.

Now: *Read through the dissertation, but avoid trying to understand it*. Forget the meaning. Look at the format. Use the checklist in the Box 9.6 and mark any mistakes and omissions with a highlighting pen.

This final check is the one stage in the writing-up *which cannot and must not be done on the word-processor*. Many of the things you are looking for, especially in relation to text and page format, may not be evident on screen (printer drivers vary in the exactness with which their output represents the screen version).

What you need to do is look at the complete, assembled document with fresh eyes. The best way to do this is to turn off the computer and take the draft to a different room where you will not be disturbed. Find a table where you can lay the pages out and look at them properly and in comfort (for example, so that you go through the citations with a pencil and tick them off in the Bibliography). Once you have marked up the mistakes, *then* you can return to the computer, edit the indicated pages and print the final copy.

Box 9.6   What to look for in the final draft

☐   Have you followed all the departmental guidelines on format?
☐   Are you within the specified number of pages or words?
☐   Are all the details on the title page present and correct?
☐   Is the Abstract completed and in the right place?
☐   Are the Acknowledgements as you want them?
☐   Are all the pages numbered consecutively?
☐   Are all the pages present and in the correct order?
☐   Is the Table of Contents complete, consistent and properly laid out?
☐   Are the Tables of Illustrations and Appendices complete?
☐   Are all citations in the text referenced in the Bibliography?
☐   Does every reference in the Bibliography have a citation?
☐   Are all the references complete in every detail?
☐   Are the references in the correct order?
☐   Are all abbreviations fully explained the first time they appear?
☐   Do all the illustrations have legends?
☐   Does each illustration have at least one reference in the text?
☐   Are all the illustrations present?
☐   Are there any unexpected changes in font size or type?
☐   Are all the line and paragraph spacings as you want them.
☐   Are there any:
     –   widows (the last line of a paragraph at the top of a page), or
     –   orphans (the first line of a paragraph at the bottom of a page)
     to be edited out?

GETTING IT IN ON TIME

Golden rule: *Find out the submission deadline for your work and have it completed **one week** beforehand.*

This (like most of the other gems of wisdom in this book!) sounds pretty obvious and barely worth stating, but there are three good reasons for needing to get your work submitted on time:

☐   You will lose marks for lateness.
☐   You have other worthwhile things you would rather be doing (sleeping, exam revision, partying, taking a holiday, getting a job, reading for pleasure).

☐   It is unprofessional not to do so.

Those reasons are listed in increasing (*sic*) order of importance. If you don't know by now about the penalties for late submission of coursework then nothing this book can say will rescue you. Professionalism, on the other hand, is something well worth stressing once again. Working to deadlines is listed in the skills table (Table 2.2 on page 19) with good reason. You will meet deadlines in virtually any job or profession you take from here on, so you might as well get used to it.

▮ TRAPS FOR THE UNWARY

Not knowing when to stop
Presenting any kind of report or product, any creation of your own, to someone else is inevitably associated with a certain degree of anxiety. Andrew Wiles, the mathematician who finally proved Fermat's last theorem after years of self-imposed academic isolation, recalled these feelings before the lecture at which his proof was presented (Singh, 1997):

> This had been part of me for seven years ... my whole working life. I got so wrapped up in the problem ... but now I was letting go. There was a feeling that I was giving up a part of me.

The fact that your work is somewhat less ambitious than Wiles' is not germane here. Your project is your creation and contains elements of your own personality buried deep within it. You want your efforts to meet with approval because rejection or dissatisfaction reflect directly on you and will reduce your own self-esteem.

Because of these feelings you may feel a reluctance to let go, to feel that if you just do that wee bit more, check it through just one more time, it will be that much closer to the perfection you crave. Well, OK, that's a laudable sentiment (even Wiles got it wrong the first time though) but you must know where to draw the line. Your dissertation will never be perfect (even if you started all over again and did everything right this time!) and the moment has now come to let it out of your grasp and present it to the world, warts and all.

Don't worry, the pangs of separation will be short-lived. They will be quickly overcome by feelings of intense relief at getting rid of the damn thing at last, not to mention the pleasure of chucking out the contents of the shoe-box (see 'Never throw anything away', Chapter 8 on page 116). You might even find yourself doing some absurd displacement activity like cleaning your room, painting your bicycle or buying some kitsch jewellery you'll never wear.

The law of inanimate malice
This law says something to the effect that:

> Man-made mechanical devices, despite their lack of con-scious awareness, choose to fail at just those moments when they are being most relied upon.

Leave some space in your schedule for your computer to throw a wobbly half-way through the final save to disk, for the photocopier to run out of toner and mangle every third sheet, and for the car battery to be flat on the morning you set off to visit the binder. These kinds of things will happen, and they are more likely to happen if you don't leave space for them to do so.

And you should prepare for animate as well as inanimate failure. Check that there isn't a bank holiday on the day you plan to go and buy your two reams of A4, that the photographer is not off to Crete for a holiday the week before you need your precious electron micrographs duplicated, and that the library is going to be open on the evening you make the final check of your bibliography.

Misplaced trust
Don't rely on others at the last minute. Even your best friends will let you down. Not deliberately, of course, but just when you need their help the most. They have their own dissertations to complete and are feeling the pressure just like you. Their easy, relaxed style hides the same anxieties as those which you are feeling. Don't depend on them to help with that final spelling check or to take your overdue books back to the library. Don't rely on them to do your last minute photocopying or pick your photos up from the photographer.

Least of all, don't trust even your closest friend to hand your thesis in for you. Friendships are valuable things. They won't be broken by say-ing 'No, sorry' from time to time. They **will** be broken, probably for ever, by a panic let-down at a crucial moment or absent-mindedness at the final hurdle.

ASSESSMENT

ASSESSMENT CRITERIA

Your project will be assessed from a number of different points of view, by different people and according to a variety of criteria. You are entitled to know, in some detail, what and who these are. Most institutions will tell you without being asked; if they don't, find out from your supervisor what to expect.

The assessment criteria which will be applied to your work can probably be divided into two groups, to do with **process** and **outcome**, as in Table 10.1. Inevitably, many of the criteria which are used are directly related to skills listed in Table 2.2 (see page 19) and they represent your assessor's view of your level of achievement in these skills.

Whether you receive a statement of your performance in individual areas or just an overall mark depends on institutional and department policies. If you are given a general grading for your work but would like to receive more specific information, ask your supervisor if it would be possible to obtain a complete transcript of marks once the examination process is over.

SECRETS OF ASSESSMENT

Although assessment criteria can be itemized in a straightforward way, describing the manner in which marks are awarded is a great deal more difficult. A dissertation is not a multiple-choice test and cannot be marked on a highly rational, point-for-point basis. However clearly the marking criteria are specified, in the end the marks are awarded by feel. Your supervisor has a view about your performance and progress which may be difficult to quantify or express and this will colour his or her judgement to a lesser or greater extent. He or she wants to make a fair assessment of your abilities but this can reflect how you have changed (developed, improved) and your potential, as well as what you actually did.

Table 10.1 Assessment criteria for student project work	
Aspects of process	*Aspects of outcome*
Quality of planning	Completeness of investigation
Quality of method	Achievement of aims
Quality of analysis	Fulfilment of brief
Maintenance of diary and/or records	Functionality of product
Attention to detail	Comprehensiveness of literature survey
Initiative	Knowledge of subject literature
Independence	Understanding of subject
Ability to work as part of a team	Quality of presentation (includes the
Persistence	quality of the dissertation/thesis and any
Diligence	other written or spoken presentation of
	your work).
	Critical ability
	Originality
	Creativity

Many markers set about their task in a way which may appear to be working backwards. The obvious approach would be to award marks according to closely specified objective criteria, add up the total and arrive at a grade. What actually happens is that, after considering the work in detail, the marker decides which *degree level* the work most closely represents. Marks are then awarded for each specified element, and then adjusted so that the total fits the prediction.

This may seem unfair and less than academically rigorous but it is actually quite reasonable. There are several excellent reasons for doing it this way:

1. None of the assessment criteria carry any inherent definition of value. How is the marker to decide whether the quality of, for example, 'written expression' should merit 2/10, 6/10, 8/10 or even 10/10? It is just not possible to balance, say, 15 mis-spelled words against two convoluted sentences or a page with no paragraph breaks.

2. The inherent unpredictability of research means that both the progress and the outcome of the project may be different from what was originally anticipated. Either the pre-set criteria will have to

be bent and adapted to accommodate these eventualities *or* the marking scheme will have to have a 'discretionary' element which can be appropriately adjusted.

3. As with Olympic diving competitions, there may be some moderation of the overall mark to take into account the perceived **degree of difficulty** of the project. This may be done either overtly (examiners and supervisors reaching a consensus view after comparing the variety of projects submitted by the class or year group), privately (an individual marker deciding for him or herself) or subconsciously (the marker making a subjective and unrecognized adjustment to his or her decision).

4. Degree grades invariably follow a non-linear scale. Your university probably uses a system which looks something like this:
   - Third class   40–49%
   - Lower second class   50–59%
   - Upper second class   60–69%
   - First class   70+%

   The justifications for such an arrangement are lost deep in the mists of academic history but it has the singular effect of clustering degree *class decisions* over a relatively small (31%) portion of the percentage scale. Given this, if assessments were carried out with perfect numerical objectivity there would be a great many more failures and firsts awarded than actually turns out to be the case. In fact, markers work to some mental picture of what each class represents. This may or may not be overtly stated but it might look like this:
   - Third class   Worthy of a degree but of poor quality
   - Lower second class   Competent
   - Upper second class   Extremely competent
   - First class   Outstanding

   (many other descriptors could be used).

In awarding a grade, the marker's intention is to make an unambiguous public statement about the quality of the student; that invariably means being subjective, whatever the numerical marks might say.

PREPARING FOR THE ORAL EXAMINATION

Oral (viva voce) examinations take different forms but usually have similar aims:

❑   To ascertain that the work is the candidate's own.
❑   To determine the extent and depth of the candidate's knowledge.
❑   To ask about aspects of the candidate's work which may be ambiguous, unusual or unclear.
❑   To ask for the correction of errors prior to acceptance.

There are some things you need to know in order to prepare properly for your oral examination:

❑   When it will be, where it will take place, how long it will last.
❑   Who will be there and who will be asking you questions (the external examiner?, an internal examiner?, your supervisor?, other staff?).
❑   Who the external examiner is and his or her subject background.
❑   The scope of the examination (your project/dissertation?, recent parts of your course?, earlier parts of your course?, exam answers?).
❑   The balance and weighting of marks to be awarded.

You have a right to be given this information beforehand and your department will probably offer it. If they do not, ask your supervisor or tutor to find out for you. On the basis of this information, you can revise appropriate material although there is a limit to the preparations you can make. The wide potential remit and short time available for each student means that it is difficult to predict the kind of questions that will be asked. You should be prepared to rely largely on your existing knowledge rather than on last minute cramming. You will want to be as familiar as possible with your dissertation, even if it was handed in some months previously. Be reassured, however, that you will probably be the only person in the examination room with a deep and thorough knowledge of its contents.

Some departments offer students the chance of a practice run prior to the oral examination. This presents an additional stress that you might feel inclined to avoid, but that would not be wise. Oral examinations are sufficiently rare and unusual events that even the most self-confident, knowledgeable and normally loquacious student can be struck dumb by the unfamiliarity of it all. Ask for an opportunity to practise and try to get some idea of how you respond under the spotlight.

Above all, you should realize that the examiners are interested in your work and are not trying to catch you out. If you find the questioning aggressive or disorientating, that may reflect your unfamiliarity with the situation or, indeed, the examiners' own nervousness. You will, naturally, be assessed on your performance. You should feel stressed but not abused. Once you leave the examination room any personal elements in the process will be forgotten by them (if not by you). The examiners want you to do the best you can and much prefer marking up to marking down.

THE EXTERNAL EXAMINER

External examiners usually carry the final responsibility for the maintenance of academic standards in the face of all this subjectivity. Degree grades comprise their own mini-language, as indicated above. The exchange of senior academic staff between institutions at assessment time ensures that the words of the mini-language retain more or less universal meanings.

Very often, the project carries more than its own weight in terms of degree grade. In other words, although the project mark forms a specified percentage of the total for the degree, the project itself may be used to assess whether students with borderline marks are worthy of being pushed up a class or grade. It will usually be the external examiner who gives the final decision, taking into account the student's performance in the viva voce examination and the advice of the supervisor and any other members of departmental staff involved in the assessment.

By this means, the subjective element in project assessment is turned to advantage and contributes to a continual re-evaluation of degree quality.

GETTING FEEDBACK

Once your research is completed and the report submitted, you may be so glad to be rid of it that the thought of getting a detailed critical assessment of your performance is unappealing. This may be the case especially if the dissertation was the last piece of coursework before your final degree examinations: you have other matters to concern yourself with and what is done is done.

On the other hand, the uniqueness of your research and the fact that your dissertation was so completely different from everything else you have done during your course may mean that you are intrigued to know how well you have performed. However friendly and informative your supervisor may have been during the doing and writing stages, you still have this nagging feeling that an objective assessment will throw up errors or inadequacies. And you may legitimately wonder whether your writing style has been convincing and professional.

There are several ways of finding out how you have done:

- ❏ During your viva voce examination, if you get the chance, ask the examiners directly what they thought. It is best to ask specific questions ('Did you find the analysis of Experiment 3 convincing?', 'Do you think I gave adequate coverage of the literature on such and such?') rather than vague, open-ended ones ('Did you like it?', 'Was it OK?'). If you can find the confidence to do this, you may be surprised at how intrigued and impressed the examiners are to have the tables turned (politely) on them in this way. Apart from anything else, this can be a means of leading the conversation on to areas which interest you and on which you feel reasonably confident.

- ❏ When all aspects of the assessment are complete, ask your supervisor to tell you what he or she thought about your work. The important thing here is timing: the response you will get once the pressure of assessment is off (on both sides) will be more objective compared with that obtained at the time of submission (when, as far as your supervisor is concerned, there is still everything to play for).

- ❏ Find out exactly *why* you have been given the mark you have been given. How was it broken down and what were the strengths and weaknesses of your work? This information is available to you on request and your examiners should be able to justify their assessment.

- ❏ Show your dissertation to someone you trust to give you a sensible, unflattering opinion. This might be particularly useful if you have studied a subject directly related to your career intentions, if you think you might want to do further research or if you think some of what you have done could be considered for publication. Perhaps there is someone in the Department other than your supervisor who knows enough about your subject to give you the objective opinion you are looking for.

- ❏ Ask someone you trust, not about the content of your dissertation but about its style and presentation. This will tell you about other aspects of your achievement and set you thinking once more about the skills which, as discussed earlier, are probably the most valuable outcome of your work. This in turn will help to prepare you for the next stage of your research project: *Shouting about it* (see Chapter 11).

DEALING WITH CRITICISM

The point was made earlier that by writing up the outcome of your research you are *objectifying* it. In other words, you are making new information accessible to others and inviting them to consider what it is that you have found out about the world. The corollary of this is that all research, at whatever level, invites criticism. This goes with the territory and has to be dealt with as unemotionally and as professionally as possible. Coping with criticism is just another valuable, adaptable skill.

In your present state of mind, however, adopting this detached approach might prove to be extremely difficult. What you want is a good degree and everyone around you is watching your performance to see if you are worthy of one. The criticism you have invited is not criticism of the information you have discovered but criticism of you. It reminds you once more of those fears and anxieties that you often felt at school. Being professional in this situation is tough.

You will come to your own method of dealing with the critical reactions to your work, whether in the form of an overall mark or more detailed comments, but the following advice may help.

❐   *Welcome and accept criticism*

The comments you receive will have been made after considerable thought and will have been offered in a spirit of helpfulness. Thank your critics politely for their useful advice (even if you feel like strangling them or jumping off a cliff).

❐   *Take time before responding*

Your first reaction to any criticism is likely to be more emotional than it should be. It is very unlikely to be the same response you would give after a bit of thought. Avoid being pressurized into an immediate response. Ask for time to think about what has been said: your critic will be impressed by this and may even be caused to reflect on the depth of argument on which the criticism was based. Remember: you know your own work better than anyone else, including the unwritten reasons why you did what you did. Get these things straight in your mind before reacting.

❐   *Don't be defensive*

An instant rebuttal may make you feel better in the short term but it doesn't really help you to come to terms with the criticism. Analyse what has been said (play at being devil's advocate for a moment) and try hard to see the point. If you find it to be justified, learn from the criticism. If you still think the criticism is unjustified you might wish to say so (politely, constructively and on the basis of factual argument) or just remain silent. Either way, the issue will have been resolved in your mind and will no longer keep you awake at night.

❐   *Try to get more than one reaction to a specific point*

An individual critic has only one individual view and may not be correct. If a point is raised unexpectedly or you don't fully understand it, discuss it with someone else and then decide how much notice you want to take of what has been said. Be especially wary of any criticism that does not seem to be backed up by reasoned argument.

To take an analogy, treat criticism as if you were a wrestler meeting a new opponent in the ring: you can't avoid what's coming so face up to it with all the skill and confidence you can muster. Recognize your own limitations but remember that your opponent has weaknesses too. If your opponent starts throwing weight around, turn that to your advantage, but at the end of the bout reflect on what you have learned. Don't lose your temper. Improve your skills in preparation for next time. You have survived, with a few bruises, but you can stay confident in your own abilities. And try to stay on reasonably good terms with your opponent: you may meet again in the future and not necessarily in the ring.

SHOUTING ABOUT IT

11

SHOUT ABOUT IT!

WHAT IS THERE TO SHOUT ABOUT?

Now that your research project is complete and you have a smartly bound dissertation sitting on the shelf, what happens next?

There are several different answers to this question, depending on your plans for what to do when you leave university, but they all involve celebrating your achievement. Obtaining your degree has been a very significant achievement; indeed, it is probably the most successful thing you have ever done. Adding those few letters to your name denotes a considerable intellectual achievement, not to mention several years of single-minded effort, of which you can be extremely proud. Now your thoughts must turn to making the most of your degree, to jobs and careers, and to trying to sell yourself to others.

Selling yourself and making the most of your skills can turn out to be surprisingly difficult. How do you set about convincing a potential employer that you have the attributes that they are looking for? How can you get through the anonymity barrier which separates you from the imaginary, perfect person they are trying to recruit? How can you make yourself stand out from the multitude in a crowded job market?

Employers recognize this difficulty, as indicated by the quotations in Box 11.1. Writing a beautifully crafted letter of application and enclosing an elegant CV is only part of the story. You need to be able to articulate your abilities, including the special achievements which your degree, and especially its research project, have engendered.

Box 11.1   The importance of selling your skills

1. Recent quotes from employers

> Students often have difficulty in articulating how they have developed and more particularly in providing evidence.

> Students may not be aware that the skills they use and take for granted should always be put down for the potential employer to be aware of.

> We are looking for the perfect candidate ... someone who is numerate, computer literate, can analyse, probe, be motivated, is a good team player, can take initiative, can lead, has excellent communication skills, understands the company and wants to contribute to its success, can own and solve a problem and has the determination to see situations through to the end.

2. How it used to be (with apologies for the dated gender assumptions!)

> What qualities, then, does the employer look for in his graduate recruits? Does he see the graduate simply as a well-equipped brain, or as a person with qualities of mind and character, who will be an asset to the firm?
> In fact it is the personal, rather than academic, qualities that influence the attitude of firms towards their graduate recruits. The chief concern of employers is to get graduates – both in arts and science – who are good mixers: men with a sense of humour, wide interests, tact, the ability to get on with people. Next in order of importance come qualities of character, such as leadership and responsibility. As one firm put it: 'They must have personality, have their feet on the ground and be good mixers. No back-room boys.'

Department of Scientific and Industrial Research (1957).

■ RECOGNIZE YOUR ACHIEVEMENTS

The ideal graduate might be described as someone who is **capable**, who can turn ideas into action. Capability ... carries within it notions of autonomy, control, expertise, imagination and skill – the skilful application of knowledge and the knowledgeable application of skills.

(Walker, 1994)

You might want to consider for a moment why people go to university. What is it about graduates that make them special? The quotation above gives one view on this, expressed in terms of capability. Here 'graduateness' implies a combination of skills and achievements, but also the qualities of maturity and independence. People who employ graduates do so because they value these capabilities and can exploit them. In return, graduates can reasonably expect to find the type of work which offers challenge, excitement, responsibility, motivation and a continually changing environment.

One of the things you will have realized, and realized especially during the last stages of your degree work, is that learning never stops. If your degree means anything at all it means that you have acquired the skills of continuing to learn. Graduates are therefore also described as 'independent learners'. As pointed out at the start of this book, one reason why your university teachers wanted you to do a research project was to encourage your independence.

Here is a recently published list of the characteristics of the independent learner. See how many of them apply to you: independent learners:

❒   enjoy learning and seek out opportunities to learn;
❒   know how they learn best and seek out these ways of learning;
❒   ask perceptive questions;
❒   contribute their own enthusiasms and ideas to the subject;
❒   can identify what is impeding their learning and take steps to overcome these obstacles;
❒   know what they already know and know what it is they still need to learn;
❒   know that they need to learn and can identify their learning needs.

(Adapted from Baume and Baume, 1997)

Look at Box 11.2. How would you describe your personality? Have you changed? What caused you to change? What contribution did the experience of research make to your personal development?

Box 11.2   Personality types

Change occurs all around us, all the time. Our response to change varies but defines elements of our personality. It is possible to respond actively (initiating developments or leading resistance against them) or passively (enjoying change or ignoring it). Your university studies will have made you appreciate that nothing, least of all your own specialist subject area, stands still. Your project will have put you in touch with that change directly and demanded that you adopt an attitude towards it.

Here are some descriptors of personality types:

❏ Innovator Someone who is never content with the *status quo*, looks for new ways of doing things, devises new approaches and tries to carry others along.

❏ Embracer Someone who is happy to be led along by an innovator, welcomes change and does their best to stay informed.

❏ Enthusiast An active embracer: someone who welcomes changes, looks for new opportunities, encourages others to change and seeks to exploit developments to their own advantage.

❏ Pragmatist A person who accepts change as inevitable, follows the crowd and gets on with the job in whatever new form it takes. A pragmatist accepts, and may even come to like, new ways of doing things but never demands or instigates change themselves.

❏ Sceptic Someone who thinks, often on principle, that change is inevitably disadvantageous and will tell others so. A sceptic takes a lot of convincing but may eventually become an embracer. For a sceptic, the development-before-last was the best.

❏ Traditionalist Someone who is largely oblivious to change and carries on working the same way that they have always done, whatever happens. This kind of person often thinks the old ways, the old certainties, were best and sees no reason to change.

❏ Resister The opposite to an embracer; someone who dislikes and actively avoids new developments but may be forced, eventually, to accept them.

They can be arranged as a continuum, on two sides of a fence:

Box 11.2	Continued			

ACTIVE: Innovator Enthusiast Sceptic Resister

†‡

PASSIVE: Embracer Pragmatist Traditionalist

Consider the following questions:

- ❑ Which personality descriptor do you feel best applies to you?
- ❑ Are you at one point on the scale or do you move around?
- ❑ How easy is it to move horizontally along the scale?
- ❑ Which side of the fence are you on?
- ❑ Might you change from one side of the fence to the other?
- ❑ Is your subject area fast or slow moving?
- ❑ What is your reaction to the changes going on in your subject?
- ❑ Do you feel a need to change from one type of personality type to another?

■ SELL YOUR SKILLS: THE SKILLS AUDIT

Go back and look at Table 2.2 on page 19. This table divided skills up into four types and suggested the particular abilities which might be put under each heading. In preparing for your job application, you will find it helpful to carry out a **skills audit** on yourself. Base the audit on this table, using headings and contents (individual skills) rearranged in any way you choose. Most importantly, list the skills you have acquired or developed using *your own terminology* and ascribe meanings to the words in a way which *you can understand*. Include skills derived from your project, but also skills that have come from other parts of your course and from other interests. You might want to make a separate list of the subject-specific skills and knowledge which you have acquired and which you think might be of special interest to an employer.

In carrying out your skills audit, don't be overly concerned with the *level* of skill which you have achieved. What you need to record is the fact of the experience rather than your level of ability. There may be exceptions to this, for example, if you have followed a certificated skills course of some kind. Generally speaking, however, the skills in the list will not be objectively assessable and your experience of them will be very individual in nature. If you are anxious about the credibility of your achievements, your university or department may provide a written statement of the skills you have developed while following individual modules or courses. Alternatively, you could ask your supervisor to do this in relation to your project and your tutor to do it for the rest of your course. They will both be very pleased to mention specific achievements or experiences when writing a job reference for you. Don't be afraid of discussing with them in advance what you would like (or not like) to have said about you.

The skills audit should provide a mass of material on which to base your job applications. As a bland list of headings, the audit table may not be all that useful to employers but it will enable you to organize what it is that you want to say about yourself. Your task now is to transform its contents into more meaningful information. Use the column headings in Table 2.2 on page 19 (process skills, management skills, etc.) as a guide and pick out some significant events or achievements which illustrate the most important skills you wish to talk about.

One thing the skills audit *will* do is put some flesh on the bare title of your dissertation. It is very unlikely that any of the people who eventually read your application form (personnel officer, recruitment agency staff, department head, team leader, etc.) will understand what your research project was about, just by reading its title. These people are probably not quite so ignorant of matters as Uncle Ebenezer (see Box 7.2 on page 111), but you would be very unwise to assume that they have more than a distant knowledge of your specialist area. They will probably also be unaware of the exact circumstances under which you carried out your project. (Even if they went to university, it was somewhere else and a long time ago.)

So use skill development as an excuse to tell them about your project. Include a very brief synopsis (no more than two or three lines) of what you did and then identify the real value which it had for you. Tell them how much time you spent on it, what opportunities it offered, how you exploited these opportunities and why this now makes you the person they are looking for.

■ USE YOUR SKILLS TO SELL YOURSELF

Here are eight suggestions which might help you to get the right job. Think about them when you are writing application letters, completing forms, making speculative phone calls or attending interviews. The precise circumstances in which you apply them will depend on the nature of the job you are looking for and the application process itself.

1. Give the impression that you can offer **long-term commitment**, that you are someone who will be able to perform effectively at work throughout the rest of your working life. There is a kind of 'white lie' being perpetrated on both sides here: you know, and your potential employer knows, that you will almost certainly move jobs quite frequently through the course of your working life (the days of gold watches for 50 years service to one employer are long gone). Nevertheless, you want the employer to feel that it is worth their while to take you on. You need a major commitment from them (security, salary, benefits, training, etc.) just as they are looking for commitment from you (loyalty, service and devotion to the interests of the organization). It is best if you both work on the assumption that these commitments will apply for a substantial period of time.

2. Show that you can be **trained**. It is most unlikely that you will leave university, enter a job, start work and be immediately productive. The knowledge and skills you have gained at university will be useful but will not be enough. The company or organization will want to train you for the function they want you to perform. This training may consist of anything from a simple induction course designed to introduce you to the company's products and way of doing things to a lengthy education or technical programme leading to a professional qualification. Whatever it is, you will only be taken on if you can prove that you are trainable and have the potential to repay (in productivity) the investment that the organization makes in you. How can you prove this? One way is to think back to the very start of your research project and the ignorant state in which you found yourself. Compare this with your present state of knowledge and skills (imagine starting the project again!) and reflect on the processes by which you got to where you are.

3. Show that you are **adaptable**. Whatever type of employment you obtain, the nature of the work you do will be subject to constant change. This may be for reasons associated with the work itself or for reasons more associated with you (Table 11.1). Changes of this kind are inevitable and the only sensible approach is to work with rather than against them. So, in looking for a job, you need to emphasize your adaptability and flexibility. You need to be seen as someone who expects things to change and welcomes new opportunities. Your project experiences provide plenty of evidence that you are this kind of person.

Table 11.1 Sources of change in the way you work	
Changes in the job	*Changes in you*
☐ Altered demand for products of services (imposed by changes in technology, the market, the economy, fashion, etc.) ☐ Demand for new skills ☐ Restructuring of the organization	☐ Altered seniority and responsibilities ☐ Altered interests and motivation ☐ Acquisition of new skills ☐ New life circumstances and personal responsibilities

4.   Show that you can **present** yourself. This advice refers to some obvious things, such as using your word-processing or DTP expertise to construct an attractive CV, turning up for interview on time and looking smart, but also to some which are less obvious, such as returning telephone calls, giving thoughtful answers to questions and appearing optimistic. Capitalize on the presentation skills you have gained: give sufficient time to preparation, focus on the needs of the audience, and get your message across.

5.   Show that you have done your **homework**. Use your research skills to get clued up about the company, its market, its product or its place in society. This doesn't need to be a mammoth effort but just enough to enable you to hold an informed conversation or ask intelligent questions at an interview. Remember the first stages of your literature review: use the same techniques of first finding the broad extent of the information followed by a more detailed look at some judiciously chosen items.

6.   Show that you can take **responsibility**. Make sure you emphasize your maturity and independence. This does *not* mean presenting yourself in an arrogant or over-knowledgeable manner but it *does* mean remembering to point out examples of where you have coped with problems, followed ideas through to the end, taken decisions or provided leadership. Your project work, as well as the rest of your degree work and your other interests will provide you with plenty of experiences to draw on. Don't be afraid of mentioning them explicitly in letters of application, in your CV or in answer to interview questions. They may not, in themselves, be directly relevant to the job you are trying to get, but they will demonstrate an essential capability.

7.   Show that you can work as part of a **team**. A team is any group of people working together. The minimum size is two, although you have almost certainly worked in teams larger than this. The

essential point about teamwork is that the outcome is of greater value than the sum of the individual contributions. You and your project supervisor comprised a team: you worked together to identify, formulate, analyse, research and investigate a problem. Perhaps other people joined in for all or part of the effort. Think about how the work tasks were identified and allocated (mostly to you!). Remember how you reviewed progress together and adjusted the strategy as you went along. Flick through your dissertation and your project diary and remind yourself of where key decisions were taken or where advice was sought. This all adds up to a valuable body of information, as far as job seeking is concerned, and is something to shout about.

8. Show that you have good **time management skills**. How did you manage, in the end, to fit your research project successfully into the rest of your academic and personal schedule? What tricks and private rules did you come up with to enable you to get everything done? How did you manage to survive the tightrope? What was it that increased the thickness of the miraculous time cake? If a second-year student came and asked you for advice, what would you tell them?

Tell your potential employer about these achievements, even if they don't ask.

WHAT ABOUT FURTHER RESEARCH?

Your project and dissertation will have given you quite strong feelings about research. These may be positive ('Loved doing it', 'Best thing since the invention of the pot noodle', 'Completely altered my way of thinking') or negative ('Hated every moment of it', 'Never again', 'Can't wait to leave and get a proper job') but they will be strong. If your feelings are positive, and if you were reasonably successful in the rest of your degree, you might want to consider opportunities for doing further research. What opportunities are there?

1. Study for a doctoral degree (PhD)
This is the traditional route towards full-time research and one which for many years has been the normal means of entering an academic career. Statistically, the number of graduates continuing directly from first (Bachelor's) degree to doctoral research is very small, but much of the activity of universities depends on a steady trickle of research

students through the system. For those committed to their subject, enthralled by knowledge, fascinated by the pursuit of understanding, fed up with assessment by examination and prepared to be both poor and single-minded for another three or four years, there is no alternative. The intellectual rewards are immense and the failure rate is very low.

Research students normally need to obtain support, either in the form of a research studentship grant (funded publicly or by the university) or by obtaining a salaried departmental post as research assistant. Either arrangement is for a limited time (usually three to four years, longer if part-time), very badly paid and dependent on the achievement of a good (Class 1 or 2:1) first degree. You will be assigned to an academic supervisor and the department will probably have some formal mechanism for checking on your progress at regular intervals. There is unlikely to be any formal programme of study but you may be given training in research methods and/or asked to attend specific undergraduate modules to fill any gaps in your knowledge.

Ask your supervisor for advice about how to find research studentships, at your present university and elsewhere. You can also look in the research and education sections of magazines, journals and newspapers. In some cases grant funding goes with the appointment; in others it has to be applied for separately. There is usually strong competition, both for places and for funds. Get advice and be persistent.

2. Study for a Master's degree

Master's degree courses are a means of continuing specialized study in your chosen subject area. In many respects they resemble the final year of a first degree, including the requirement for a research project. Master's courses usually last a full calendar year, have a large proportion of formal study and usually culminate in written examinations. Sometimes they have a strong element of practical training and lead to a vocational certification. A good first degree in a related subject is a usual prerequisite. Grant funding comes in a number of different forms and usually has to be applied for competitively.

The research project for a Master's degree may have to be completed over the whole year or may be condensed into a period of intense study covering a limited number of weeks or months. There are many similarities between Master's and Bachelor's research projects, including the production of a written dissertation, and much of the advice offered in this book is applicable to both. The biggest difference is likely to be in the intensity of the work required: for example, the Master's student will be expected to complete a significant piece of research in a very short time without many of the concurrent learning opportunities available to undergraduates. In other words, he or she is usually expected to be already in possession of effective research skills, not to mention sound time management techniques and other personal skills. The experience of the first degree project will have provided most of these capabilities but students embarking on a Master's course should expect a year of exceptionally hard work.

As with PhD research, there are many intellectual gains to be had by pursuing your subject one step further in this way. The year will fly by, but you are likely to emerge with a specific, vocationally relevant qualification which improves your employment prospects. A Master's degree can also be a stepping stone to a research studentship. Both degrees have the effect of deepening rather than broadening your specialist knowledge and that is something to bear in mind if you want to keep your career options as open as possible. Discuss these matters with your careers advisor, your supervisor, your tutor and anyone else whose experience and wise counsel you can trust.

3. Using research at work

If you are keen to get a proper job, but still find the notion of research appealing, there are many opportunities available. You will have realized from your work so far that the 'research team' consists of many individuals operating at many different levels of responsibility and making many different kinds of contribution to the collective effort. This is true in universities but it is equally true in commercial companies and publicly funded organizations of all kinds. The 'product', whether it be tangible, functional, financial, social, intellectual, theoretical, creative or artistic, has to be imagined, designed, tested and reviewed – exactly those processes which your research project entailed.

Now that you know what research really is, you will have no trouble in spotting where it is carried out. If you keep an open mind and positive attitude, you will quickly develop the skill of reading between the lines of job adverts and employment specifications to find the information you want. Somewhere out there is a job which depends on the processes and values of research. As an experienced researcher, that is just the kind of job you would be good at.

BIBLIOGRAPHY

Alley, M. (1987), *The Craft of Scientific Writing*, Prentice-Hall, Englewood Cliffs, NJ.
Advice on how to get scientific thoughts across to the reader. Plenty of examples of how and how not to do it.

Allison, B., O'Sullivan, T., Owen, A., Rice, J., Rothwell, A. and Saunders, C. (1996), *Research Skills for Students*, Kogan Page, London.
A practical guide to research and experimental design, especially in the social sciences and humanities. Gives guidance on sampling methods, questionnaire design and interview techniques. Based on exercises and activities. Available as a paperback or as a folder of worksheets.

Avery, H., Strath, L., Taylor, K., James-Cavan, K., Taylor, C., Tromly, A. and Brown, S. (1989), *Thinking it Through: A Practical Guide to Academic Essay Writing*, Academic Skills Centre, Trent University, Ontario.
Offers guidance on the fundamental skill of converting thoughts into written words.

Baume, C. and Baume, D. (1997), 'The art of inspiring independent learning', *The New Academic* **6** (3) 2–6.

Bell, J. (1993), *Doing your Research Project: A Guide for First-Time Researchers in Education and Social Sciences*, 2nd Ed., Open University Press, Buckingham.

Berry, R. (1994), *The Research Project: How to Write it*, 3rd Ed., Routledge, London.
A guide to writing (rather than researching) research essays, particularly in the humanities. Offers a guide to library use, a specimen paper and a useful appendix on the avoidance of sexist language.

Blaxter, L., Hughes, C. and Tight, M, (1996), *How to Research*, Open University Press, Buckingham.
A research guide aimed at all researchers, not just those in academic institutions. Contains exercises, case studies and extensive, annotated bibliographies. Useful for advice on collecting and analysing data, especially in the social sciences and education.

Brown, S., McDowell, L. and Race, P. (1995), *500 Tips for Research Students*, Kogan Page, London.
Advice in bite-sized chunks. Mainly intended for PhD students or others embarking on an academic career but may be worth dipping into.

Buzan, T. (1995), *The Mind Map Book*, BBC Books, London.
The classic book on Mind Mapping®; makes you wonder why you didn't think of it yourself. Easy to read and generously seasoned with intriguing illustrations.

Creme, P. and Lea, M.R. (1997), *Writing at University: A Guide for Students*, Open University Press, Buckingham.
Discusses what is meant by 'academic' writing and looks at various styles to be adopted for written university assignments. Helpful hints on planning written work and the actual process of writing.

Department of Scientific and Industrial Research (1957), 'Graduates in British Industry', findings of a study by Political and Economic Planning, Department of Scientific and Industrial Research.

Drew, S. & Bingham, R. (1997), *The Student Skills Guide*. Gower Publishing, Aldershot.
A practical student guide to study skills, built around tried and tested worksheets developed at Sheffield Hallam University. Provides advice at 'starter' and 'development' levels. Useful at all undergraduate levels and beyond.

Entwistle, N. (1998), 'Motivation and approaches to learning: Motivating and conceptions to teaching,' in Brown, S., Armstrong, S. and Thompson, G. (eds.), *Motivating Students*, SEDA/Kogan Page, London, 15–23.

Fairbairn, G.J. and Winch, C. (1996), *Reading, Writing and Reasoning: A Guide for Students*, 2nd Ed., Open University Press, Buckingham.
Deals with the essential processes listed in its title in an approachable and readable manner. Particularly helpful on organizing thoughts and turning them into organized text.

Fowler, H.R., Aaron, J.E. and Longman, N.Y. (1998), *The Little, Brown Handbook*, 7th Ed., Longman, New York, NY.
A modern, thorough but easily understood reference guide to style, grammar and effective writing. Loaded with examples and explanations.

Gibbs, G., Rust, C., Jenkins, A. and Jaques, D. (1994), *Developing Students' Transferable Skills*, Oxford Centre for Staff Development, Oxford.
Intended as a guide for staff and course designers but illustrates the importance of transferable skills and suggests ways of developing them. Useful bibliography.

Greenhalgh, T. (1997), *How to Read a Paper: The Basis of Evidence-based Medicine*, BMJ Publishing Group, London.
A guide to using the medical literature and to interpreting the scientific basis of medicine. Contains plenty of practical advice on obtaining, evaluating and using medical literature, plus exercises. Highly readable by anyone interested in the nature of evidence, its presentation, interpretation and exploitation.

Henry, J. (1994), *Teaching Through Projects*, Kogan Page, London.
A teachers' guide to the use of projects in teaching, particularly in open and distance learning courses.

Kirkman, J. (1992), *Good Style: Writing for Science and Technology*, E. & F.N. Spon, London.
A lively and engaging guide to effective writing. Considers how style can be adapted to the needs of the audience, with plenty of amusing examples of failure (don't miss pp. 86–90!). Explains, in simple terms and with examples, the art of making your writing readable.

Kolb, D.A. (1984), *Experiential Learning*, Prentice-Hall, Englewood Cliffs, NJ.

Lewis, V. and Habeshaw, S. (1997), *53 Interesting Ways to Supervise Student Projects, Dissertations and Theses*, Technical and Educational Services Ltd, Bristol.

Lumley, J.S.P. and Benjamin, W. (1994), *Research: Some Ground Rules*, Oxford University Press, Oxford.
A wide-ranging reference manual offering the practical keys to success in all types of research and its presentation. Particularly helpful sections on statistics, ethical issues and health and safety.

Márquez, G.G. (1997), 'Hacks in the time of tape recorders', speech to the Inter-American Press Association, quoted in *The Observer*, 25 May, 1997.

Martin, P. and Bateson, P. (1993), *Measuring Behaviour: An Introductory Guide*, 2nd Ed., Cambridge University Press, Cambridge.
Don't be put off by the title. Although aimed at a particular discipline, this book is a goldmine of practical advice on the planning, design and execution of experimental projects. Written in a crystal clear style and very readable.

Mepham, T.B. (1966), 'Ethical analysis of food biotechnologies: an evaluative framework,' in Mepham, T.B. (ed.), *Food Ethics*, Routledge, London, 101–119.

McArthur, T. (1996), *The Oxford Companion to the English Language*, Oxford University Press, Oxford.

Newstead, S. (1998), 'Individual differences in student motivation', in Brown, S., Armstrong, S. and Thompson, G. (eds.), *Motivating Students*, SEDA/Kogan Page, London, 189–199.

O'Connor, M. (1991), *Writing Successfully in Science*, Chapman and Hall, London.
Advice for scientists on writing successful research papers.

Orna, E. and Stevens, G. (1995), *Managing Information for Research*, Open University Press, Buckingham.
A useful, well illustrated reference guide to methods of handling information. Deals with how to obtain, record and digest the information needed to carry out good research as well as how to present your own findings in the most effective manner. Has particularly valuable chapters on the practicalities of page and document design.

Palmer, R. (1993), *Writing Style: A Guide to Good English*, E. & F.N. Spon, London.
A completely unstuffy guide to good writing for essays, reports, letters and more. Sprinkled with memorable principles to follow and equally memorable cartoons. Explains and illustrates the rules of grammar that frightened you at school. Don't leave home without it.

Pechenik, J. and Lamb, B. (1994), *How to Write about Biology*, Harper-Collins, London.
Aimed at biologists at all levels; covers everything from examinations and lab reports to research papers and oral presentations.

Popper, K.R. (1972), *Objective Knowledge: An Evolutionary Approach*, Oxford University Press, Oxford.

Purchell, K. and Pitcher, J. (1996), *Great Expectations: The New Diversity of Graduate Skills and Aspirations*, Higher Education Careers Services Unit, Manchester.
A survey of graduate skills and experiences from the point of view of careers advisors. Gives an insight into the needs and expectations of employers and how students perceive the skill development value of their courses.

Sagan, C. (1997), *Billions and Billions*, Headline, London.

Sharp, J.A. and Howard, K. (1996), *The Management of a Student Research Project*, 2nd Ed., Gower Publishing, Aldershot.
Partly a practical study guide and partly an academic treatise on student research, this book is aimed at student researchers at all levels but particularly postgraduates; undergraduates should read it selectively. Introduces and contrasts different types of research activity. Somewhat heavy on management processes, with several daunting flowcharts, but provides a useful insight into the theory of research.

Singh, S. (1997), *Fermat's Last Theorem*, Fourth Estate, London.
A gripping story of how an age-old mathematical conundrum was eventually solved. Insight into the mathematical way of doing things. Thoroughly readable by ordinary mortals.

Strath, L., Avery, H. and Taylor, K. (1993), *Notes on the Preparation of Essays in the Arts and Sciences*, 4th Ed., Academic Skills Centre, Trent University, Ontario.

Temple, M. (1997), *Grammar Book*, John Murray, London.
Only 99p. Buy it!

Turabian, K.L. (1996), *A Manual for Writers of Term Papers, Theses, and Dissertations*, 6th Ed., University of Chicago Press, Chicago.
A valuable reference manual on all aspects of form and format in academic writing. Reliable and informative although the second comma in the title betrays its US orientation. Concentrates on the mechanics of presentations as well as advising on prose style.

Turk, C. and Kirkman, J. (1989), *Effective Writing: Improving Scientific, Technical and Business Communication*, 2nd Ed., E. & F.N. Spon, London.
A valuable source of practical guidance on written presentation. Also considers the most effective ways of illustrating what you have to say.

Walker, L. (1994), 'The British Context,' in *Institutional Change Towards an Ability-based Curriculum in Higher Education*, Oxford Brookes University/Employment Department, 8–11.

Williams, K. (1996), [The 'Developing Writing' series] (1) *Essential Writing Skills*, (2) *Using Data*, (3) *Scientific and Technical Writing*, (4) *Writing Reports*, (5) *Writing Essays*, Oxford Centre for Staff and Learning Development, Oxford.
A series of modestly priced, workshop-style guides with examples and illustrations. Lively, practical and informative. Highly recommended.

INDEX

Effective Literature Searching for Students

Sarah Gash

This practical guide will greatly assist final year and post-graduate students who as part of their research for a dissertation or thesis, must carry out an exhaustive search of the existing printed and electronic literature sources. Most students will have done a certain amount of literature searching to prepare for earlier course work, but this will often not have gone farther than the library catalogue. The principles of a systematic approach are explained, suggestions are made for planning, carrying out and recording the search, obtaining the material discovered, preparing a bibliography and correctly citing the references.

Although intended primarily for students, academic staff involved in research and supervisors of research projects will also find it helpful.

Gower

MBA Management Models

Sue Harding and Trevor Long

If you're a student on an MBA or management course, you'll be
expected to demonstrate a knowledge of a range of models.

This textbook collects together the 45 models most likely to be
required, summarized in a standard format. Each entry contains a
diagram of the model; the principles on which it's based;
underlying assumptions; guidance on application, and relevant
issues; related models; and sources of further reference. Models are
organized by subject area: accounting; business strategy; human
resources; organizational strategy; and strategic marketing. An
alphabetical matrix index facilitates the process of finding the right
model quickly.

MBA Management Models will be invaluable to students working on
written assignments, projects, case studies or dissertations, and to
practising managers too.

Gower

Student IT Skills

Mark Pettigrew and David Elliott

This book presents a completely new approach to learning and developing IT skills. It is based on experience of how people really learn, has been tested with real students and then rewritten to take their observations into account.

Readers are encouraged to learn IT by doing and by guided exploration, and build their confidence to explore and develop further. They are helped to:

• choose relevant and suitable real world tasks
• find out how their software, whatever it is, can perform the tasks
• increase their confidence in the use of IT
• further develop their IT skills by exploration.

As readers explore, they are encouraged to develop a framework of understanding. The practical skills, along with this framework, form a powerful, self-reinforcing way of learning about IT.

Gower

The Student Skills Guide

Sue Drew and Rosie Bingham
Learning and Teaching Institute
Sheffield Hallam University

Thousands of students have helped in the development of this uniquely practical book, designed to guide you as you extend the range of skills you need to complete your chosen course of study successfully.

Structured, straightforward guidance is given on the following topics:

Identifying Strengths and Improving Skills
Organising Yourself and Your Time
Note Taking
Gathering and Using Information
Essay Writing
Report Writing
Oral Presentation
Group Work
Solving Problems
Negotiating and Assertiveness
Coping with Pressure
Revising and Examination Techniques

The interactive style of the chapters enables you to produce a tailor-made plan for each skill that is best suited to your way of working, yet incorporates the essential elements required for success. This approach has already proved its worth to thousands of students who participated in the extensive trialling and improvement process for this guide that was undertaken in one of the UK's largest universities over a three year period leading up to its publication. All their advice, feedback and input has been incorporated into this book, together with the suggestions of teaching staff from around the country.

Anyone wishing to establish firm foundations for a range of skills that will not only improve course results, but also future employment prospects, will find this guide invaluable.

Gower